Day Wal

PembrokesnireCoast

20 routes in
south-west Wales

Vertebrate Publishing, Sheffield
www.v-publishing.co.uk

Day Walks on the PembrokeshireCoast

20 routes in
south-west Wales

Harri Roberts

Day Walks on the PembrokeshireCoast

20 routes in south-west Wales

VP First published in 2018 by **Vertebrate Publishing**.

Vertebrate Publishing, Crescent House, 228 Psalter Lane,
Sheffield S11 8UT, United Kingdom.
www.v-publishing.co.uk

A CIP catalogue record for this book is available from the British Library.

ISBN 978-1-910240-98-4

Front cover: Looking north from Carn Llidi, near St Davids Head (route 11).
Back cover: Sunset from St Govan's Head (route 3).
Photography by **Adam Long** unless otherwise credited. www.adamlong.co.uk

All maps reproduced by permission of Ordnance Survey on behalf
of The Controller of Her Majesty's Stationery Office.
© Crown Copyright. 100025218

Design by Nathan Ryder, production by Jane Beagley.
www.**v-publishing**.co.uk

Printed and bound in Europe by Pulsio.
Vertebrate Publishing is committed to printing on paper from sustainable sources.

MIX
Paper from
responsible sources
FSC® C128169
www.fsc.org

Contents

* Shortcut available

MOUNT SION DOWN, CASTLEMARTIN RANGES

Introduction

The Pembrokeshire Coast National Park is one of the smallest of Britain's national parks and the only specifically coastal park. Its breathtaking scenery, comprising rugged cliffs, sandy beaches and sheltered coves, is accessible to walkers via the Pembrokeshire Coast Path. One of three designated National Trails in Wales (and forming part of the Wales Coast Path), this long-distance trail traces almost every twist and turn of the 299 kilometres (186 miles) of Pembrokeshire coast, from St Dogmaels in the north to Amroth in the south.

Unsurprisingly, most of the walks in this guide (sixteen in total) are coastal in nature and incorporate parts of the Pembrokeshire Coast Path. The range of maritime landscapes encountered is astonishing and varies considerably from one region to the next.

Pembrokeshire's south coast is best known to visitors, with its resorts and popular sandy beaches. There is nevertheless great variety here and parts of the Angle Peninsula are as wild and unspoilt as anywhere in the national park. The Bosherston Lily Ponds are a must-see, while the Castlemartin Peninsula contains some of the most dramatic limestone cliffs in Britain.

Dominating Pembrokeshire's western coast is the large, crescent-shaped bay of St Brides. Along both 'arms' of the bay are dramatic cliffs and small sheltered coves, including one of the finest natural harbours in Wales at Solva. The smaller Dale Peninsula provides two contrasting coastlines: east on to the sheltered waters of Milford Haven and west into the stormy Atlantic Ocean.

In general, Pembrokeshire's north coast is more rugged and demanding. There are rocky coastal hills formed by ancient volcanoes and steep slopes rising into the Preseli foothills. Dinas Island is a rugged, sloping promontory rising to over 140 metres, while tectonic movements between Newport and St Dogmaels have cracked and contorted the cliffs into a series of dramatic coastal features.

Two distinct areas – the Daugleddau estuary and the Preseli Hills – showcase some of Pembrokeshire's inland treasures. The first of these is a classic example of a ria, or submerged river valley, characterised by mudflats, salt marsh and steep wooded shores. This enclosed and tranquil landscape is quite unlike any other in Pembrokeshire.

The Preseli Hills extend from Mynydd Dinas in the west to Crymych in the east. Connecting the main line of hills is an ancient trackway known as the Golden Road and the whole area is dotted with prehistoric remains. The steep-sided Gwaun valley carves its way into the uplands, forming a ribbon of green woodland between the bare treeless hills.

There are many classic Pembrokeshire walks which appear time and again in guides to the area. I have not ignored these but I have also tried to include some less well-known routes, away from the coast. Even if you have walked in Pembrokeshire before, I hope this book will provide a fresh perspective on the county and lead you to places you have yet to discover.

Harri Roberts

Acknowledgements

As ever, I would like to thank my partner, Tracy Burton, for casting an experienced editorial eye over the finished typescript, providing cheer and company on the walks themselves, and for not complaining – too much – when the weather took a turn for the worse.

About the walks

The walks described in this guide are between 6.5 and 12.9 miles (10.4 and 20.8km) in length and will take around 3.5 to 7 hours to complete at a leisurely pace. For all but two of the walks shortcuts providing less demanding routes have been suggested. These are clearly marked on the map and in the route description.

On the whole, the walks follow clear waymarked trails (including the Pembrokeshire Coast Path) through fields, woodland, coastal common and upland, as well as along tracks and quiet country lanes. Where a walk uses an undefined path or route finding is difficult, this is mentioned in the summary for the walk. It is always a good idea to study this carefully, along with the detailed route description, before setting out.

Although the walks vary in terms of length and difficulty, they should all be within the capabilities of a reasonably fit walker. Bear in mind, however, that a number of walks contain lengthy and strenuous ascents. Where appropriate, alternative routes have been described to reduce the amount of overall height gain.

Navigation

As a rule, the description and map included should be enough to get around safely and accurately, but it's always worth carrying a backup copy of the relevant OS map, in case you inadvertently travel off the page, or need to change your route for any reason.

The routes in this book are covered by the following maps:
OS Explorer OL35 North Pembrokeshire (1:25,000)
OS Explorer OL36 South Pembrokeshire (1:25,000)

GPS

A GPS can be a useful navigational aid and is well worth carrying. But always carry spare batteries – they do tend to run out at the worst times – and always carry a map and compass as backup.

Mobile phones

Mobile phone reception can be patchy along the coast, with signals often blocked by cliffs or steep-sided valleys. If you do need to make contact with emergency services, try heading inland or up on to a cliff, where you often have more chance of a signal.

Footpaths and rights of way

The walks in this book all follow rights of way, permissive paths or cross open access land.

Comfort

A decent pair of boots will protect your feet from the kind of terrain experienced in the hills and will also provide ankle support, waterproofing and grip on steep slopes. And a waterproof jacket could be useful on any day at any time of year. A pack containing a waterproof, spare layer and some food and drink will make any day more comfortable. Anybody with joint problems, for example ankles or knees, will probably benefit from a pair of trekking poles.

Safety

Walking in coastal areas comes with a set of specific dangers. Stay away from cliff edges, which may be unstable, and avoid informal paths leading down to beaches. Check the weather forecast before you set out, and also tide times if necessary. Tide times for the next seven days can be found at **www.tide-forecast.com**

Mountain rescue

In case of an emergency dial **999** and ask for **Police** and then **Mountain Rescue**. Where possible give a six-figure grid reference of your location or that of the casualty. If you don't have reception where you are, try and attract the help of others around you. The usual distress signal is six short blasts on a whistle every minute. If you don't have a whistle, then shouting may work.

Coastguard rescue service

In the event of a coastal emergency, dial **999** and ask for the **Coastguard**. Where possible give a six-figure grid reference of your location or that of the casualty. This information can be found on almost every stile and gate along the Pembrokeshire Coast Path. If you don't have reception, try to attract the attention of others around you, either by shouting or through the use of a whistle.

Emergency rescue by SMS text

In the UK you can also contact the emergency services by SMS text – useful if you have low battery or intermittent signal. You need to register your phone first by texting **'register'** to 999 and then following the instructions in the reply. **Do it now** – it could save yours or someone else's life. **www.emergencysms.org.uk**

MOD closures

Parts of the Pembrokeshire coast are owned by the Ministry of Defence (MOD) and are subject to access restrictions. These are mentioned where relevant in the instructions for each walk. The only route seriously affected is Walk 3, Bosherston & Stackpole, which crosses part of the Castlemartin Training Area frequently closed for weapons testing. Monthly firing notices can be downloaded from **www.milfordmarina.com** or phone **01646 662 367** for daily updates (firing schedules can change without warning). When firing is taking place, prominent red warning flags are flown around the perimeter of the danger area.

Traveline Cymru

Two of the walks described in this guide – Walk 2, Lamphey to Tenby, and Walk 9, St Davids to Newgale – are linear routes requiring the use of public transport to return to your starting point. If planning to follow one of these walks, it is recommended that you check out the latest public transport information by visiting the Traveline Cymru website – **www.traveline.cymru** – or phoning their helpline on **0800 464 00 00**.

The Countryside Code

Respect other people

Please respect the local community and other people using the outdoors. Remember your actions can affect people's lives and livelihoods.

Consider the local community and other people enjoying the outdoors
» Respect the needs of local people and visitors alike – for example, don't block gateways, driveways or other paths with your vehicle.
» When riding a bike or driving a vehicle, slow down or stop for horses, walkers and farm animals and give them plenty of room. By law, cyclists must give way to walkers and horse riders on bridleways.
» Co-operate with people at work in the countryside. For example, keep out of the way when farm animals are being gathered or moved and follow directions from the farmer.
» Busy traffic on small country roads can be unpleasant and dangerous to local people, visitors and wildlife – so slow down and, where possible, leave your vehicle at home, consider sharing lifts and use alternatives such as public transport or cycling. For public transport information, phone Traveline on 0871 464 00 00 or visit **www.traveline.cymru**

Leave gates and property as you find them and follow paths unless wider access is available

» A farmer will normally close gates to keep farm animals in, but may sometimes leave them open so the animals can reach food and water. Leave gates as you find them or follow instructions on signs. When in a group, make sure the last person knows how to leave the gates.

» Follow paths unless wider access is available, such as on open country or registered common land (known as 'open access' land).

» If you think a sign is illegal or misleading, such as a *Private – No Entry* sign on a public path, contact the local authority.

» Leave machinery and farm animals alone – don't interfere with animals even if you think they're in distress. Try to alert the farmer instead.

» Use gates, stiles or gaps in field boundaries if you can – climbing over walls, hedges and fences can damage them and increase the risk of farm animals escaping.

» Our heritage matters to all of us – be careful not to disturb ruins and historic sites.

Protect the natural environment

We all have a responsibility to protect the countryside now and for future genera-tions, so make sure you don't harm animals, birds, plants or trees and try to leave no trace of your visit. When out with your dog make sure it is not a danger or nuisance to farm animals, horses, wildlife or other people.

Leave no trace of your visit and take your litter home

» Protecting the natural environment means taking special care not to damage, destroy or remove features such as rocks, plants and trees. They provide homes and food for wildlife, and add to everybody's enjoyment of the countryside.

» Litter and leftover food doesn't just spoil the beauty of the countryside, it can be dangerous to wildlife and farm animals – so take your litter home with you. Dropping litter and dumping rubbish are criminal offences.

» Fires can be as devastating to wildlife and habitats as they are to people and property – so be careful with naked flames and cigarettes at any time of the year. Sometimes, con-trolled fires are used to manage vegetation, particularly on heaths and moors between 1 October and 15 April, but if a fire appears to be unattended then report it by calling **999**.

Keep dogs under effective control

When you take your dog into the outdoors, always ensure it does not disturb wildlife, farm animals, horses or other people by keeping it under effective control. This means that you:
» keep your dog on a lead, or
» keep it in sight at all times, be aware of what it's doing and be confident it will return to you promptly on command
» ensure it does not stray off the path or area where you have a right of access

Special dog rules may apply in particular situations, so always look out for local signs – for example:
» dogs may be banned from certain areas that people use, or there may be restrictions, byelaws or control orders limiting where they can go
» the access rights that normally apply to open country and registered common land (known as 'open access' land) require dogs to be kept on a short lead between 1 March and 31 July, to help protect ground-nesting birds, and all year round near farm animals
» at the coast, there may also be some local restrictions to require dogs to be kept on a short lead during the bird breeding season, and to prevent disturbance to flocks of resting and feeding birds during other times of year

It's always good practice (and a legal requirement on 'open access' land) to keep your dog on a lead around farm animals and horses, for your own safety and for the welfare of the animals. A farmer may shoot a dog which is attacking or chasing farm animals without being liable to compensate the dog's owner.

However, if cattle or horses chase you and your dog, it is safer to let your dog off the lead – don't risk getting hurt by trying to protect it. Your dog will be much safer if you let it run away from a farm animal in these circumstances and so will you.

Everyone knows how unpleasant dog mess is and it can cause infections, so always clean up after your dog and get rid of the mess responsibly – 'bag it and bin it'. Make sure your dog is wormed regularly to protect it, other animals and people.

Enjoy the outdoors

Even when going out locally, it's best to get the latest information about where and when you can go. For example, your rights to go on to some areas of open access land and coastal land may be restricted in particular places at particular times. Find out as much as you can about where you are going, plan ahead and follow advice and local signs.

Plan ahead and be prepared

You'll get more from your visit if you refer to up-to-date maps or guidebooks and websites before you go. Visit **naturalresources.wales** or contact local information centres or libraries for a list of outdoor recreation groups offering advice on specialist activities.

You're responsible for your own safety and for others in your care – especially children – so be prepared for natural hazards, changes in weather and other events. Wild animals, farm animals and horses can behave unpredictably if you get too close, especially if they're with their young – so give them plenty of space.

Check weather forecasts before you leave. Conditions can change rapidly especially on mountains and along the coast, so don't be afraid to turn back. When visiting the coast check for tide times on **www.ukho.gov.uk/easytide** – don't risk getting cut off by rising tides and take care on slippery rocks and seaweed.

Part of the appeal of the countryside is that you can get away from it all. You may not see anyone for hours, and there are many places without clear mobile phone signals, so let someone else know where you're going and when you expect to return.

Follow advice and local signs

Wales has about 33,000km (20,750 miles) of public rights of way, providing many opportunities to enjoy the natural environment. Get to know the signs and symbols used in the countryside to show paths and open countryside.

How to use this book

This book should provide you with all of the information that you need for an enjoyable, trouble-free and successful walk. The following tips should also be of help:

» We strongly recommend that you invest in the relevant maps listed above on page viii. These are essential even if you are familiar with the area – you may need to cut short the walk or take an alternative route.

» Choose your route. Consider the time you have available and the abilities/level of experience of all members of your party – then read the Safety section of this guide.

» We recommend that you study the route description carefully before setting off. Cross-reference this with your map so that you've got a good sense of general orientation in case you need an escape route. Make sure that you are familiar with the symbols used on the maps.

» Get out there and get walking!

ABOVE PRESIPE, NEAR MANORBIER (ROUTE 2)

Maps, descriptions, distances

While every effort has been made to maintain accuracy within the maps and descriptions in this guide, we have had to process a vast amount of information and we are unable to guarantee that every single detail is correct. Please exercise caution if a direction appears at odds with the route on the map. If in doubt, a comparison between the route, the description and a quick cross-reference with your map (along with a bit of common sense) should help ensure that you're on the right track. Note that distances have been measured off the map, and map distances rarely coincide 100 per cent with distances on the ground. Please treat stated distances as a guideline only.

Ordnance Survey maps are the most commonly used, are easy to read and many people are happy using them. If you're not familiar with OS maps and are unsure of what the symbols mean, you can download a free OS 1:25,000 map legend from **www.ordnancesurvey.co.uk**

Here are a few of the symbols and abbreviations we use on the maps and in our directions:

 ROUTE STARTING POINT   ROUTE MARKER   SHORTCUT

 OPTIONAL ROUTE   52 ADDITIONAL GRID LINE NUMBERS TO AID NAVIGATION

PB = Public bridleway
GR = Grid reference
RHS/RH = Right-hand side/Right-hand

PF = Public footpath
LHS/LH = Left-hand side/Left-hand

Km/mile conversion chart

Metric to Imperial

1 kilometre [km]	1,000 m	0.6214 mile
1 metre [m]	100 cm	1.0936 yd
1 centimetre [cm]	10 mm	0.3937 in
1 millimetre [mm]		0.03937 in

Imperial to Metric

1 mile	1,760 yd	1.6093 km
1 yard [yd]	3 ft	0.9144 m
1 foot [ft]	12 in	0.3048 m
1 inch [in]		2.54 cm

Welsh place names

The vast majority of place names in the south of Pembrokeshire are English or Scandinavian in origin, due to the successful colonisation of this area by the Normans and their followers during the medieval period. However, Welsh place names predominate in the north of the county and knowing what these mean can be a great help when walking. In the following list are some of the more common place-name elements you are likely to come across, with a particular emphasis on coastal features.

aber – estuary, confluence
afon – river
allt – wood, slope
bach/fach – small
bae – bay
blaen – head of a valley
bryn – hill
bwlch – pass or gap
cae – field
caer/gaer – fort, fortified camp
capel – chapel
carn/garn – cairn or pile of stones
carreg/garreg – stone
castell – castle
cefn – ridge
cei – quay
coch/goch – red
coed – wood
craig/graig – crag
cwm – valley
dŵr – water
dyffryn – valley
eglwys – church
ffordd – road
ffynnon – well or spring
glan/lan – bank or shore
glyn – deep valley
goleudy – lighthouse
gwaun/waun – moorland or meadow
harbwr – harbour
hen – old
isaf – lower
llan – church, sacred enclosure

llwyn – bush or grove
llyn – lake
maen – stone
maes – field
mawr/fawr – big
moel/foel – bare hill
môr – sea, ocean
morfa – salt marsh
mynydd – mountain
nant – stream
ogof – cave
pant – hollow
parrog – pebble bank, flat land by sea
pen – top or end
penrhyn – headland
pentre – village
plas – hall, mansion
pont/bont – bridge
porth – harbour
pwll – pool
rhiw – slope
rhos – moorland
rhyd – ford
tan/dan – below
ton/don – wave
traeth – beach
tref/dref – homestead or town
trwyn – nose; point, cape
tŷ – house
tywyn – sandy shore, sand dunes
y, yr – the
ynys – island

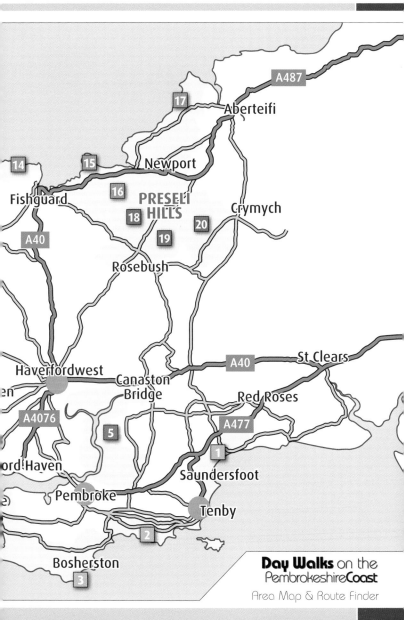

Day Walks on the
Pembrokeshire**Coast**

Area Map & Route Finder

SECTION 1

South Pembrokeshire Coast

The south coast of Pembrokeshire, between Amroth in the east and the entrance to Milford Haven in the west, is often considered gentler and less wild than the northern and western coasts of the national park. There is some truth to this, particularly along the heavily settled coastline between Amroth and Tenby. Having said that, parts of the Angle Peninsula are as wild and unspoilt as anywhere in the national park, while the Castlemartin Peninsula between Bosherston and Freshwater West contains some of the most dramatic limestone cliffs in Britain. Variety and diversity are perhaps the keynote, with a landscape that varies from rugged cliffs and beautiful sandy bays to steep-sided, wooded valleys and even artificial lagoons.

LOW TIDE AT FRESHWATER WEST (ROUTE 4)

SUNSET FROM ST GOVAN'S HEAD (ROUTE 3)

01 Saundersfoot Bay

12.2km/7.6miles

Industrial heritage in a fabulous coastal setting.

Saundersfoot » Coppet Hall » Churchton » Sardis » Pleasant Valley » Summerhill » Colby Woodland Garden » Amroth » Wisemans Bridge » Coppet Hall » Saundersfoot

Start

Pay-and-display car park adjacent to Saundersfoot Harbour.
GR: SN 136048.

The Walk

For much of the nineteenth century the seaside village of Saundersfoot served as the principal port for a thriving coal and iron industry. Coal, pig iron and firebricks would be loaded on to ships in the harbour and return laden with stone used as ballast. On this walk we explore the industrial heritage of Saundersfoot Bay more thoroughly while also enjoying fabulous coastal views.

Beginning at Saundersfoot Harbour, we follow a former railway line through a tunnel in the cliff to Coppet Hall then head inland along a field path known as the Black Walk – the route used to transport coal down to the sea before the opening of Saundersfoot Harbour in 1829. The path takes us up to St Issell's Church and on to a country lane leading up past Hean Castle to Sardis.

Dropping into Pleasant Valley, we enjoy easy walking along a former railway line as far as the Kilgetty Iron Works, an important industrial site worth exploring further. Another site of note, set in an attractive wooded valley on the far side of Summerhill, is the National Trust property of Colby Woodland Garden. This was also a key mining area from the 1790s onwards and another former railway line leads us gently down to the coast at Amroth.

Here we join the Pembrokeshire Coast Path, which follows a former coach road over the cliffs to Wisemans Bridge and then the old railway line back to Saundersfoot Harbour. However, if the tide is out we can also choose to follow the beach as far as Wisemans Bridge. Here we can study coal seams in the cliffs and even (at very low tides) the remains of a sunken forest submerged by rising sea levels over 5,000 years ago.

SAUNDERSFOOT BAY

DISTANCE: 12.2KM/7.6MILES » **TOTAL ASCENT:** 328M/1,076FT » **START GR:** SN 136048 » **TIME:** ALLOW 4 HOURS » **SATNAV:** SA69 9HE » **MAP:** OS EXPLORER OL36, SOUTH PEMBROKESHIRE, 1:25,000 » **REFRESHMENTS:** PLENTY OF CHOICE IN SAUNDERSFOOT; ROUTE ALSO PASSES THE BOTHY TEA ROOM, COLBY WOODLAND GARDEN; THE AMROTH ARMS, THE PIRATE RESTAURANT, AND THE SMUGGLERS BAR & GRILL, AMROTH; THE WISEMANS BRIDGE INN, WISEMANS BRIDGE; AND COAST RESTAURANT, COPPET HALL » **NAVIGATION:** EASY AND WELL MARKED.

Directions – Saundersfoot Bay

❻ From the car park, join the village street called The Strand; this runs parallel to the coast with the sea to your right. Join a tarmac path at the end of the road and follow it through a tunnel in the cliff face. Emerge in the car park for the Coppet Hall Beach Centre.

2 **Bear left** towards a road and cross to a kissing gate leading into a field. Follow a clear grassy path up through the field to another kissing gate and join a track. **Bear left** passing to the right of a house called Maryland, and **keep ahead** through a caravan park to reach a junction with a road opposite St Issell's Church.

3 **Turn right** and climb along a shaded lane for some 500m until you reach a T-junction. **Turn left** for a further 100m or so, then **turn left** again on to a road signed to *Sardis* and *Kilgetty*.

4 After a further 500m you will reach the hamlet of Sardis. After passing a number of houses on the left, **turn right** on to a narrow dead-end lane signed as a footpath. Just past a bench at the end of the lane, with the sea visible ahead, **bear left** through a kissing gate into a field.

5 **Turn right** and follow the field boundary past a house to another kissing gate. Cross a track to a stile into a field and **turn left**. Follow the field boundary downhill to a stile in the corner. **Keep ahead** in the next field towards a metal gate and join a track past farm buildings.

6 The track shortly turns to tarmac. **Keep ahead** at a right-hand bend, crossing a field above caravans to reach a stile and gate. Follow a path across a field and steeply downhill through woods. Emerge on a lane and **turn right**, still descending. Meet a surfaced track just past Tramway Cottage.

☻ For a shorter walk, **turn right** and follow the former tramway down to the coast at Wisemans Bridge. **Turn right** to rejoin the main route along the Pembrokeshire Coast Path back to Saundersfoot.

01 **SAUNDERSFOOT BAY**

Directions – Saundersfoot Bay continued ...

7 **Turn left** and follow the level track – a former tramway – up the wooded Pleasant Valley. After about 1km you will meet a road opposite Mill House. Cross to a footpath sign at the far end of the garden (between Mill House and Harvest Mill).

> **OR** It's worth continuing up the road for a few more metres to check out the remains of Kilgetty Iron Works on the left.

8 Cross the garden to the start of a sunken path climbing steeply **to the left** through thick woods. Where the path divides, **turn sharp right** to continue climbing. Emerge on a lane to the right of a house.

9 **Turn left**, towards a triangle of grass, then take the lane heading uphill **to the right**. As the lane levels off, you will pass some houses on the right. Immediately before the first house on the left, Green Plains Bungalow, **turn left** on to a gravel track. Follow this as far as a left-hand bend, then **turn right** on to a sunken path below trees.

KNIGHTS' WAY, AMROTH

10 The path joins a track by Cwmrath Farm. Continue up the track to a T-junction with a road and **turn right**. A few metres ahead, immediately before the *Summerhill* sign, **turn left** on to a track signed as a bridleway. Descend to a house then **keep ahead** on to a sunken track (stepped in places and possibly muddy). Continue downhill into a wooded valley, **turning sharply right** where a smaller path continues ahead and then **sharp left** to emerge on a gravel track. Keep **straight ahead**, crossing a bridge to the right of a ford, and shortly you will reach a road.

11 **Bear right** and follow the road past Rose Cottage to a signed footpath **on the right** leading into Colby Woodland Garden (directly past the tea room). Continue down a wide track along the bottom edge of steep wooded slopes. Where a track joins from the right, **bear slightly left** and continue down the valley. Join a lane descending into Amroth and emerge on the seafront by the Amroth Arms.

12 **Turn right** along the seafront road, passing shops, a cafe and a pub. At the end of the beach, join the signed coastal path **to the right** of the public toilets and climb steeply through woods. Emerge in a field, still climbing but now less steeply. The grassy path appears to continue straight ahead, but watch out for a waymarked gate **on the right** leading on to a tarmac path (a former coach road). Join this and **turn left**, eventually emerging on a road by houses.

> **OR** At low tide, it is also possible to follow the beach below the cliffs from Amroth, rejoining the coast path at Wisemans Bridge.

13 Continue **ahead** down the hill to a junction with a wider road. **Bear left** and descend towards the sea, passing the Wisemans Bridge Inn at the bottom of the hill (this road can be busy so **take care**). Follow the road along the front and then up the hill for a short distance, as far as some benches **on the left**.

14 Join a tarmac footpath and cycleway (another former tram road) hugging the coast. Follow the path through a long lit tunnel and then a much shorter one. Emerge outside the Coppet Hall Beach Centre. **Keep ahead** along the driveway, then take a signed tarmac path **on the left**. Rejoin your outward route through a third tunnel and along the village street leading to Saundersfoot Harbour.

LOOKING DOWN ON PRESIPE, NEAR MANORBIER, FROM THE COAST PATH

02 **Lamphey to Tenby** 19.1km/11.9miles

A linear walk along the beautiful south Pembrokeshire coast.

Lamphey » Freshwater East » Swanlake Bay » Manorbier Bay » Skrinkle Haven » Lydstep Haven » Giltar Point » Tenby

Start

Free car park outside Lamphey Village Hall. GR: SN 017005.

The Walk

The ever-changing 'cliffscape' between Freshwater East and Tenby with its beautiful bays and coves is without doubt a coastal walker's paradise. Unfortunately, the linear nature of the coastline and the low-lying agricultural land behind it make devising satisfactory circular walks in this area difficult.

However, with a little planning it is possible to make use of the regular rail/bus service between Tenby and Lamphey (a little over two kilometres inland from Freshwater East) and enjoy this stretch of coast without compromise. Except on Sundays, shorter walks are also a possibility, with the option of stopping or getting off the bus in Penally, Lydstep or Manorbier. Before setting out, check out the latest public transport information on the Traveline Cymru website (see page xi).

The full route begins in Lamphey, following a path and quiet lane to Freshwater East.

A lovely stretch of coast leads to Manorbier, described by the twelfth-century historian and cleric Gerald of Wales (who was born in Manorbier Castle) as 'the most pleasant spot in Wales'.

Continuing onwards, we pass the Neolithic burial chamber of King's Quoit and swap the red sandstone cliffs of Manorbier for the spectacular limestone formations of Skrinkle Haven and Lydstep Point. From Lydstep Haven, a splendid bay formed along a fault or downfold in the band of Carboniferous limestone, we continue eastwards towards Giltar Point, the closest point on the mainland to Caldey Island, before dropping down on to South Beach for a relaxing stroll into Tenby.

Tenby, with its medieval centre and brightly coloured Georgian stucco houses, is one of the prettiest and most interesting towns in Wales, and before catching your return train or bus it is strongly recommended that you allow time to explore its higgledy-piggledy streets more thoroughly.

LAMPHEY TO TENBY

DISTANCE: 19.1KM/11.9MILES » **TOTAL ASCENT:** 575M/1,886FT » **START GR:** SN 017005 » **TIME:** ALLOW 6 HOURS » **SATNAV:** SA71 5PB » **MAP:** OS EXPLORER OL36, SOUTH PEMBROKESHIRE, 1:25,000 » **REFRESHMENTS:** PLENTY OF CHOICE IN TENBY; ALSO PUBS IN LAMPHEY, FRESHWATER EAST AND LYDSTEP HAVEN, AND JUST OFF THE MAIN ROUTE IN MANORBIER AND PENALLY » **NAVIGATION:** EASY AND WELL MARKED.

SOUTH BEACH, TENBY

CONT. ON PAGE 14

Pembrokes...
Parc C...

02 **LAMPHEY TO TENBY**

Directions – Lamphey to Tenby

From the village hall car park, follow the road about 100m **to the right**, until just past a house called Tŷ Newydd. **Turn right** at a footpath sign and join a grassy track alongside a recreation ground. Follow the waymarked path across a railway and along the left-hand edge of a field. Cross a stile on to a main road.

2 Keep **straight ahead** on to a shaded lane opposite and climb steadily for about 1km. At the top of the hill, follow the lane round a left-hand bend to a fork. Take the road **on the right**, which descends briefly before climbing again. About 650m after the fork, reach a T-junction with Jason Road.

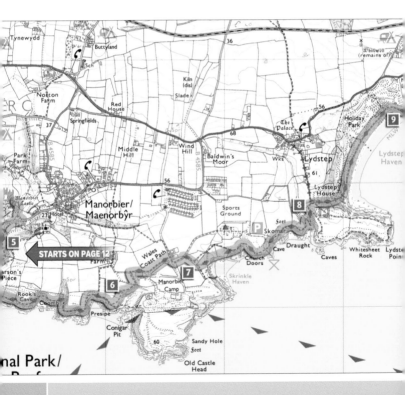

02 **LAMPHEY TO TENBY**

3 **Turn left** and follow the road down past the Freshwater Inn and through Freshwater East village. **Ignore** any paths towards the coast until you reach a small parking area **on the right** where the road bears left. **Bear right** across the car park to a footpath sign marked *To the coast path*. Follow this path down to a junction with the Pembrokeshire Coast Path.

4 **Turn left** and follow a pleasant undulating path as far as Swanlake Bay. Climb steeply out of the bay before continuing along a more level path towards Manorbier. Approaching the bay, pass in front of rental cottages and join a tarmac drive up the hill. Just past the entrance gates to the property, **bear right** on to a path between hedges. Pass **to the right** of a parking area and descend towards the beach. A concrete slab has been placed across the small stream running into the bay.

> **OR** Immediately after the stream, you may want to **turn left** to visit Manorbier Castle and St James's Church or to access the public toilets adjacent to the main car park. If you want to cut your walk short, you can also continue up the road to the village, where you will find a pub, a cafe and a bus stop.

5 Continue along the top of the beach to steps at the far end. Back up on the cliffs, the path passes a Neolithic burial chamber called King's Quoit and a number of deep, narrow fissures extending into the cliff face. At the next bay, Presipe, access to a sandy beach is possible via a steep flight of steps.

6 Old Castle Head is on MOD land with no public access, so the coast path turns inland from behind Presipe to bypass Manorbier Camp. After crossing a field to a gate in the corner, follow the security fence around until you reach a road opposite a house. **Turn right** and then **immediately left** on to a road signed to the youth hostel. Go through a gate **on the right** and follow the security fence back towards the coast.

7 Back on the cliffs, the waymarked path **bears left**, passing behind Skrinkle Haven and the smaller adjacent Church Doors Cove (a long flight of steps down to the latter provides the only safe access to either beach). Beyond the access point, **keep right** at a fork and climb steeply to an excellent vantage point overlooking the coves. The path continues past a car park before descending steeply into a narrow limestone gorge. **Turn left** up a long flight of steps.

8 At the top of the steps, take the path **to the left** and shortly emerge at a junction of tracks close to a holiday park (the path on the right can be used to follow a circular trail around Lydstep Point if desired). **Keep ahead** to the main lane and **turn right** (turning left will take you up to the village of Lydstep). Descend through woodland along the edge of the holiday park to the beautiful Lydstep Haven. Join the beach where indicated and follow it along to steps at its northern end.

> **OR** During certain high tides the beach may not be passable and you will need to follow an alternative signed route along the road through the holiday park. Rejoin the main route past the chalets numbered 491–493.

9 Climb back on to the cliffs and continue eastwards via Proud Giltar and Valleyfield Top. Approaching Penally, the coast path crosses open grassy clifftops, eventually reaching a gate leading on to MOD property. Unless the red flag is flying, **continue ahead** along the grassy clifftops towards Giltar Point.

> **OR** If the red flag is flying, you will need to take the path running alongside the fence **on the left**. This passes under the railway and emerges on the main road in Penally. **Turn right** along the main road until you reach a footpath sign **on the right** just past the railway station (you can also choose to end your walk here). Follow the path through the dunes and out on to South Beach. **Turn left** towards Tenby to rejoin the main route.

10 Follow the path **sharp left** at Giltar Point and across sandy clifftops overlooking South Beach. Pass above a former quarry and descend through woodland to the beach. Follow the expanse of sand northwards towards Tenby for close to 2km. A walkway and steps lead up from the South Beach Shack to Tenby's Esplanade, from where you can make your own way across Tenby to the bus/railway station or embark upon a more thorough exploration of the town.

SUNSET FROM SADDLE HEAD

Stunning cliffs and beaches and the famous Bosherston Lily Ponds.

Bosherston » St Govan's Chapel » St Govan's Head » Broad Haven » Stackpole Head » Barafundle Bay » Stackpole Quay » Eight-Arch Bridge » Bosherston

Start

National Trust pay-and-display car park in Bosherston. GR: SR 966948.

The Walk

The cliffs between Linney Head and Stackpole Head contain some of the best and most spectacular coastal limestone scenery in Britain. Here can be found a dazzling array of coastal formations: coves, bays, stacks, arches, chasms and headlands, as well as other features associated with limestone cliffs such as caves.

We join the coast to the east of the main Castlemartin Training Area, at St Govan's Head, where MOD access restrictions are less stringent (though be aware that the lane between Bosherston and St Govan's Head may be closed for firing, particularly during the week). From the clifftop car park a flight of steps descends along a narrow passage in the cliffs to a tiny medieval chapel – built, according to tradition, on a site established in the sixth century by St Govan.

Back on the cliffs, we cross the level coastal plateau – flattened by the sea's erosive power some five million years ago when sea levels were at least fifty metres higher than they are today – towards St Govan's Head, a wonderful vantage point from which to admire the full splendour of the adjacent cliffs. Continuing east along the coast, we encounter two hidden gems, the sandy bays of Broad Haven and Barafundle, and another spectacular limestone headland, Stackpole Head.

At Stackpole Quay, a tiny harbour built in the late eighteenth century to export limestone, we say goodbye to the coast and head inland across Stackpole Park to reach the eastern arm of the beautiful Bosherston Lily Ponds. This series of shallow, interconnected lakes, rich in wildlife, was created at the turn of the nineteenth century by the owner of the Stackpole Estate, Baron Cawdor. Their tranquil wooded shores are a stark contrast to the wildness of the nearby coast and provide the perfect end to a memorable walk.

BOSHERSTON & STACKPOLE

DISTANCE: 14.1KM/8.8MILES **»** **TOTAL ASCENT:** 272M/892FT **»** **START GR:** SR 966948 **»** **TIME:** ALLOW 4.5 HOURS **»** **SATNAV:** SA71 5DN **»** **MAP:** OS EXPLORER OL36, SOUTH PEMBROKESHIRE, 1:25,000 **»** **REFRESHMENTS:** YE OLDE WORLDE CAFE AND ST GOVAN'S COUNTRY INN, BOSHERSTON; THE BOATHOUSE CAFE, STACKPOLE QUAY **»** **NAVIGATION:** EASY AND WELL MARKED.

BROAD HAVEN

03 BOSHERSTON & STACKPOLE

Directions – Bosherston & Stackpole

❻ From the car park, walk back up to the road and **turn left**, passing Ye Olde Worlde Cafe and St Govan's Inn. Take the road **bearing right** signed to St Govan's and after about 600m cross a cattle grid on to MOD land. The lane continues for another kilometre or so to reach a clifftop car park. Go through a gate and keep **straight ahead** to reach steps in the cliff signed to *St Govan's Chapel*.

> **OR** Access to St Govan's Head may be restricted due to military firing (ring 01646 662 367 for daily updates), in which case you will need to join the coast path at Broad Haven. There are a number of possible routes, but the most straightforward is to take the lane **forking left** at the southern end of Bosherston village. This is signed to *Broad Haven* and ends in a car park near Trefalen Farm. Take the path down to the beach to rejoin the main route.

2 Climb back up the steps from the chapel and **turn right** on to a tarmac track across the clifftop. After roughly 300m, this **curves right** and follows the cliffs out to an impressive vantage point on St Govan's Head. Retrace your steps to a junction with a gravel track passed earlier and **turn right**.

3 After leaving MOD property, the track becomes a path running across grassy clifftops. Stick to the main path and avoid being drawn too close to the cliff edge. With Broad Haven visible ahead, go through a wooden gate **on the left** and join a clear path leading through coastal scrub. **Bear left** towards a car park then **turn sharp right** on to a surfaced path. Descend to a beautiful sandy beach and **turn left**.

4 From the eastern end of the beach, it's possible to scramble up low sandy cliffs to the continuation of the coast path above. However, the official route follows the beach inland to cross a bridge over a stream. **Keep ahead** to a junction and take the path **on the right** signed to *Stackpole Quay*.

> **☞** For a much shorter walk, **keep ahead** along the Alternative Coast Path signed to *Bosherston*. This follows the **right-hand edge** of one of the lily ponds to Grassy Bridge. Cross over and **turn left** to rejoin the main route.

5 The trail climbs across loose, sandy terrain with no one clear path until you dip down to a kissing gate above the beach. A grassy path then leads out to Saddle Point at the end of the bay. Continue along open grassy clifftops, passing a huge sinkhole (Sandy Pit) and a large coastal fissure (Raming Hole). Follow the cliffs **to the right** to walk around Stackpole Head, then head back inland until you reach a gate leading into woodland. Descend through the trees to another beautiful sandy bay, Barafundle.

> If time is short, it's possible to avoid the loop around Stackpole Head by keeping **straight ahead** on to a grassy path across the neck of the headland. This rejoins the main route at the gate leading into the woods above Barafundle.

6 Cross the sandy beach to steps on the far side and climb to an old archway in an estate boundary wall. Follow the path across another grassy clifftop and then down the hill towards Stackpole Quay. **Turn left** at a junction of paths near the bottom of the hill, then immediately **fork left** on to a higher, woodland path alongside an over-grown wall (i.e. **ignore** the path dropping down to the road). Pass toilets and the Boathouse Tearoom and emerge in a large car park.

7 **Keep ahead** to the top of the car park and join a gravel track leading up to a metal field gate. Go through this and follow the track continuing **straight ahead** between large open fields – use the obvious plastic handles to remove and replace any electric fences. A little over a kilometre or so after leaving the car park, the track descends to cross Eight-Arch Bridge on the eastern arm of the Bosherston Lily Ponds.

8 On the far side of the bridge, take the path to the **immediate left** and follow the wooded shore of the lake as far as Grassy Bridge. Do not cross the bridge/dam, but keep **straight ahead** along a rougher track, climbing gently and passing round a **right-hand bend**. Take a path **forking left** signed to *Bosherston* and drop back down to the lake.

9 Cross a bridge over the lily pond and climb steps to an open grassy area with good views. After dropping back down to the lake, the path continues along the shore to another bridge **on the left**. Cross this and keep ahead on to a path climbing away from the lake. **Keep right** at a fork and shortly emerge back in the car park in Bosherston.

THORN ISLAND AND WEST ANGLE BAY

16.2km/10.1miles

A wild, rugged peninsula at the entrance to Milford Haven.
Freshwater West » West Angle Bay » Angle » Freshwater West

Start

Small free car park off the B4319 at
the northern end of Freshwater West.
GR: SM 884004.

The Walk

The Angle Peninsula, a narrow finger of
land jutting out between Freshwater West
and Angle Bay, forms one side of the
entrance into the Milford Haven waterway
(the Dale Peninsula forms the other). On
the peninsula's southern shores, facing
the open sea, the coast is wild and unspoilt;
the northern coast, lapped by the gentle
waters of Milford Haven, has a more civi-
lised feel. It is also exposed to the impact of
modern industrial activity, with views to
the east dominated by the extensive para-
phernalia of the oil industry: pipes, jetties
and smoking refinery towers.

Freshwater West, the dramatic sweep of
sandy beach from which we begin our walk,
couldn't be more different. Between here
and West Angle Bay the coast path is as
tough as it gets, dropping and climbing

steeply on narrow, sometimes exposed
paths as it negotiates several steep-sided
valleys. Our reward is the wild, unspoilt
scenery noted above.

After passing Thorn Island, with its Victorian
fort, we follow the northern edge of the
peninsula above Milford Haven. There are
some great views, despite the scars of
modern industry visible to the east. The
waterway, described by Admiral Nelson as
'the finest port in Christendom', is a classic
example of a ria or submerged river valley
flooded by rising sea levels at the end of
the last ice age.

Before heading back to Freshwater West,
our route takes us around Angle Bay –
a sheltered expanse of mud and sand popular with waterfowl and wading birds – and
through the village of Angle. This former
fishing village was founded in the medieval
period and its single street of cottages is
still backed by a series of long, narrow fields,
a legacy of the manorial farming system.

ANGLE PENINSULA

DISTANCE: 16.2KM/10.1MILES » **TOTAL ASCENT:** 445M/1,460FT » **START GR:** SM 884004 » **TIME:** ALLOW 5.5 HOURS » **SATNAV:** SA71 5AH » **MAP:** OS EXPLORER OL36, SOUTH PEMBROKESHIRE, 1:25,000 » **REFRESHMENTS:** WAVECREST CAFE, WEST ANGLE BAY; THE COOKHOUSE CAFE, CHAPEL BAY FORT; THE OLD POINT HOUSE AND THE HIBERNIA INN, ANGLE » **NAVIGATION:** EASY AND WELL MARKED.

Thorn Island
(ANGLE C)
Hotel

4

West Angle Bay

MLW

MLW

3

West Pill

Chapel Bay
Fort
(dis)

5

Chapel
Bay

Chapel B

Spr

Angl

Lowrey's
Rock

East Block House
(remains of)
Rat
Island

PC

North Studdock
Cottage

North
Studdock

B 4320

53

52

Waterfall

Castles Bay

Tor

South
Studdock

Spr

Airfield
(disused)

58

Whitedole
Bay

Parsonsquarry
Bay

Sheep Island

Pembrokeshire Coast Path

Guttle Hole
(Natural Arch)

Cave

01

West Pickard
Bay

East P

84

85

86

Popton Point

Fort Popton

IRB & LB Sta

6 Angle Point

Sewage Works

Jetty

Sawdern Point

Sawdern

Castle Farm

Five Ridge

The Hall

Sand & Mud

Angle Bay

MLW

Lodge

MHW

Wales Coast Path

Bangeston Wood

Spr

Carters Green

Bangeston

53

Hardings Hill

Middlehill

Broomhill

8

Rocket Cart House

61

Broomhill Cottage

B 4320

Resr

Sprs

Dunes

Black Cave

Gravel Bay

2

88

War Meml

The Devil's Quoit Burial Chamber

Dunes

Tumulus

Kilpaison Burrows

87

89

The Hoary Rocks

Broomhill Burrows

Pit

Pembrokeshire Coast Path

SURFING

Freshwater West

04 ANGLE PENINSULA

Directions – Angle Peninsula

➎ Follow the path from the car park down towards the beach as far as a waymark post. **Turn right** on to a path through the dunes. After a brief climb, the path drops into a dip with a wooden gate to the right – this is the path you will use to return to Freshwater West at the end of the walk.

2 **Keep left** and the coast path continues around the Angle Peninsula, climbing and descending steeply several times. After about 6km, you will pass the former gun emplacements at East Block House. The path then **bears right**, leaving the cliffs to descend along field edges into West Angle Bay.

> **➋** From West Angle Bay, the walk can shortened by omitting the coastal circuit of North Hill and following the road directly to Angle. Walk up through the village, past the Hibernia Inn, and rejoin the main route just past St Mary's Church.

3 Keep **straight ahead** through the car park at West Angle Bay and on to a gravel track. **Ignore** an unmarked path on the left between concrete pillars; the correct path, which is waymarked, **forks left** a bit further along, on a right-hand bend, and itself immediately forks. Take the **right-hand** path to continue around the coast (the left-hand path leads to a viewpoint overlooking West Angle Bay).

4 Approaching Thorn Island, the path **bears right** and climbs high above the north shore of the peninsula along Milford Haven. When the path is not hemmed in by hedges, there are distant views of extensive pipes and jetties extending far out into the waterway. A **right turn** takes the path to the right of Chapel Bay Fort and out to a junction with a tarmac lane.

5 **Keep ahead** past the fort car park on to a track. Pass cottages. Just before the track ends in a field, **fork left** on to a waymarked path into woodland. After leaving the trees, **keep ahead** along the left-hand edge of fields until you join an enclosed path. Descend towards Angle Point, crossing the access track to Angle Lifeboat Station.

6 Beyond Angle Point the path **curves right**, along the bottom of a field, into Angle Bay, and shortly emerges on a track in front of The Old Point House pub. **Keep ahead** along the track and follow the shore round to a junction with Angle's main village road, a short distance **to the left** of St Mary's Church.

At low tide, it is possible to walk directly across the bay along a shingle bank known as 'The Ridge'. This is signed as a bridleway, but be aware that the shingle only extends part of the way across the bay. The crossing is only advised for those who enjoy splashing around in mud!

Turn left along the village street, **continuing ahead** at the end of the houses on to a dead-end lane and later a private drive just above the shore. Where the drive turns inland to the right, **keep ahead** along the signed coast path for about 100m, then **turn sharply right** on to a path through the woods. Rejoin the lane by a former lodge house and **bear left**. Climb steadily for roughly 700m until you reach a T-junction with the main road from Angle.

Turn left along the road for about 350m. Approaching the distinctive tower of the Rocket Cart House (a former coastguard watchtower and now holiday cottage), **turn right** at a signed footpath through a gate and walk down the right-hand edge of a field towards the sea. In the next field, the path **bears half left** down to a gate at the bottom of the field, though crops may require you to deviate from the direct route. A path continues down through scrub to a junction with the coast path. **Turn left** and retrace your steps back to Freshwater West.

Wet crops and mud can make the field path between the Rocket Cart House and the coast unpleasant after bad weather. The path can be avoided by continuing along the road for a further 500m then **turning right** on to a road signed to *Freshwater West*. Pass a war memorial overlooking the bay and descend steeply to return to the car park.

FRESHWATER WEST

SECTION 2

Daugleddau

The Daugleddau estuary is formed by the confluence of the Eastern and Western Cleddau rivers (the name literally means 'the two Cleddaus') and is a classic example of a ria or submerged river valley flooded by rising sea levels at the end of the last ice age. The upper reaches of the Daugleddau, along with the tidal stretches of both Cleddau rivers, the Cresswell and Carew rivers, and other smaller tidal creeks and inlets, form a small but unique part of the national park characterised by mudflats, salt marsh, and steep wooded shores alternating with gently sloping farmland – an enclosed and tranquil landscape sometimes known as 'the secret waterway'.

LOOKING UP CASTLE REACH ABOVE LAWRENNY QUAY (ROUTE 5)

ST CARADOG CHURCH, LAWRENNY

05 Landshipping Quay & Lawrenny

Tidal waters and ancient woodland in the heart of Pembrokeshire.

Landshipping Quay » Sam's Wood » Coedcanlas » Lawrenny Wood » Lawrenny Quay » Lawrenny » Burnett's Hill » Landshipping Quay

Start

Lay-by at Landshipping Quay by memorial to mining disaster. SN 009109.

The Walk

For much of the nineteenth century, Landshipping Quay on the Daugleddau river was the centre of a thriving coal-mining venture, combining mines and shipping port in one location. All that is left to recall those times today is a memorial to those who lost their lives in Pembrokeshire's worst mining disaster, in February 1844, when at least forty men (and, almost certainly, numerous women and children under ten working underground illegally) were killed when the tunnels they were working in below the Daugleddau collapsed and flooded.

Our walk begins at this sobering memorial before tracing the shores of the Daugleddau southwards towards Lawrenny Quay (spring tides may affect shoreline paths near Sam's Wood and along Garron Pill). The route we follow passes through an attractive mix of fields and woodland, but the undoubted highlight is Lawrenny Wood, an ancient oak woodland managed by the National Trust that hugs the steep slopes overlooking the Daugleddau between Garron Pill and the Cresswell river.

Leaving the woods, we enter Lawrenny Quay, an idyllic spot popular with boaters and a good place on a fine day to stop for a drink or bite to eat by the estuary. From the quayside, a permitted path takes us over the hill to the picturesque village of Lawrenny and provides great views along the Cresswell river before we emerge below the well-preserved twelfth-century parish church.

The remainder of our walk follows mainly quiet country lanes and takes us past the restored Burnett's Hill Chapel. This was built in 1812 to serve the local mining community but, like so many Welsh chapels, closed in the 1980s for want of a congregation. Bought by the national park authority, the chapel was restored in 2001 with the help of a Lottery Fund grant and is well worth a look inside.

LANDSHIPPING QUAY & LAWRENNY

DISTANCE: 14.6KM/9.1MILES » **TOTAL ASCENT:** 269M/883FT » **START GR:** SN 009109 » **TIME:** ALLOW 5 HOURS » **SATNAV:** SA67 8BE » **MAP:** OS EXPLORER OL36, SOUTH PEMBROKESHIRE, 1:25,000 » **REFRESHMENTS:** QUAYSIDE TEA ROOMS AND LAWRENNY ARMS, LAWRENNY QUAY; THE LAWRENNY COMMUNITY SHOP, LAWRENNY » **NAVIGATION:** MAINLY EASY AND WELL MARKED BUT WITH NO CLEARLY DEFINED PATH ALONG SHORELINE AND IN FIELDS.

Directions – Landshipping Quay & Lawrenny

➍ From the lay-by, **turn right** and follow the lane across Landshipping Bridge and up the hill. **Fork right** through a metal field gate where the lane turns to track and continue until you reach a gate ahead marked *Private*.

2 Just before the gate, **turn right** over a stile leading down to the Daugleddau foreshore. **Turn left** and follow the edge of the estuary past a house and along to the start of Sam's Wood **on your left**. Where indicated, enter the woods through a gate.

3 Climb through trees to a wooden gate and **turn right**. The path contours across a steeply wooded slope then climbs steps **to the left**. **Bear right** at the top of the steps and emerge in a field. **Keep ahead** along the left-hand field edge to a corner then follow the hedge downhill **to the right** to reach a gate and stile leading on to a lane **on the left**.

4 Continue up the road ahead, reaching a T-junction after about 250m. **Turn right** and enter Coedcanlas, following the road **sharply right** and then **left**. About 100m after the left-hand bend, **turn right** through a kissing gate into a field.

5 Head **diagonally left** across the field to a stile, then continue **straight ahead** across the middle of a second field to reach a kissing gate on the far side (the gate is initially concealed by a slight rise). **Turn right** on to a lane and descend past Chapel Cottage on a left-hand bend and into a wooded dip. As the road emerges from the dip, **turn right** over a stile and join a woodland path ascending to the left.

  ◑ For a shorter route, continue along the lane for a further 800m or so as far as Knowle Cross Roads. Rejoin the main route by **turning left** at the crossroads on to the lane signed to *Landshipping* and *Martletwy*.

6 The path soon leaves the woods, crossing a stile into a field. **Turn right** and follow the field edge to a corner and then back along **to the left**. Where the field edge turns downhill to the right, keep **straight ahead** across the field to a stile on to a track and **turn left**.

05 LANDSHIPPING QUAY & LAWRENNY

7 Almost immediately, **bear right** and cross a stile into a field. Follow the bottom, right-hand edge of the field below Southernpits Farm, using the plastic handles to remove and replace any electric fences across the way. Continue along the field boundary as it drops **to the right** then climbs back up the hill **to the left**. **Ignore** the first stile on the right (into the grounds of a house) and continue up to a second, waymarked stile. Join an enclosed grassy path and shortly emerge on the access track to Garron.

8 **Bear left** to a junction with a lane and **turn right**. Cross Garron Pill and **turn right** at a footpath sign along the foreshore. Leave the shore where indicated up steps into Lawrenny Wood and follow the path **to the right**. After passing a birdwatching hut, the path starts to **bear left**, along the main Daugleddau estuary. Continue across steeply wooded slopes as far as Lawrenny Quay.

9 **Turn left** at a junction with a track and keep **straight ahead** into a boatyard. **Bear right** in the yard and drop down towards the Quayside Tea Rooms on the estuary front. Follow the road to the left until just past the The Lawrenny Arms.

10 **Fork left** on to a woodland path and climb to a field at the top of the hill. **Keep ahead** along the top left-hand edge of two fields, estuary views to your right, then enter a third field via a kissing gate. Descend **to the right** then pass through a gap in the field boundary **on your left**. Follow the top edge of a field until just below the parish church. **Bear left** through a waymarked gap and cross a field to a kissing gate in the far corner, just below the churchyard.

11 Emerge on to a road and **bear left** (for the community shop and centre of village, **turn right**). Follow the road out of Lawrenny and back down to Garron Pill. This time, continue **straight ahead** up the hill. After about 500m, you will reach a crossroads.

12 Keep **straight ahead** up the hill, following signs for *Landshipping* and *Martletwy*. About 1.2km after the crossroads, **ignore** a lane on the right and descend gently to Curly Wells Bridge. After a brief climb, the road turns sharp left and shortly passes Burnett's Hill Chapel. **Keep ahead** at a *Give Way* sign just past the chapel.

13 Where the lane turns sharp left, **continue ahead** on to a gravel track. Use a grassy track to cut off a corner then rejoin the gravel track as far as the entry gate to a house. Go through a small wooden gate **to the right** of the gate marked *Private* and follow the fenced-off path along the edge of the grounds.

14 Beyond the house, enter a field and continue along the top right-hand edge. Follow the field edge as it **bears right** to a corner and then back along **to the left**. With woods ahead, go through a gate/gap **on your right** and **turn left** to follow the field boundary along the edge of the woods. Two fields later, emerge on a track opposite a stone cottage and **turn right**. Descend all the way back to the lane at Landshipping Quay and **turn right** to return to your starting point.

FOOTBRIDGE NEAR GARRON PILL PHOTO: TRACY BURTON

SECTION 3

West Pembrokeshire Coast

The west coast of Pembrokeshire is dominated by the large, crescent-shaped bay of St Brides, which extends for almost 15 kilometres (9 miles) as the gull flies between Ramsey Island in the north and Skomer Island in the south. Both 'arms' of the bay – the St Davids Peninsula in the north and the Marloes Peninsula in the south – are characterised by dramatic cliffs and small sheltered coves, including one of the finest natural harbours in Wales at Solva. South of St Brides Bay, the smaller Dale Peninsula provides two contrasting coastlines: east on to the sheltered waters of Milford Haven and west into the stormy Atlantic Ocean.

COAST PATH ABOVE MUSSELWICK SANDS, LOOKING NORTH TOWARDS TOWER POINT (ROUTE 7)

LIFEBOAT STATIONS AT PORTSTINIAN (ROUTE 10)

ST ANN'S HEAD LIGHTHOUSE

06 Dale Peninsula

10.9km/6.8miles

Sheltered bays and windswept cliffs on a beautiful peninsula.

Dale » Castlebeach Bay » Watwick Point » Watwick Bay » West Blockhouse Point » Mill Bay » St Ann's Head » Westdale Bay » Dale

Start

Pay-and-display car park in Dale.
GR: SM 811058.

The Walk

The bulbous shape of the Dale Peninsula creates an obvious circular walk that is never out of sight or sound of the sea. Our starting point in Dale is on the sheltered, eastern end of a shallow glacial valley crossing the thin, 'pinched' neck of the peninsula. Between Dale Point and Musselwick Point, the curve of the coast creates a perfect natural harbour which helped make Dale one of the most important ports in Pembrokeshire during the sixteenth century and continues to attract the sailing fraternity in droves.

From Dale we follow the lane out towards Dale Fort, now a field studies centre for marine biologists, before joining the coast path proper along the sheltered wooded slopes behind Castlebeach Bay. Further south, at West Blockhouse Point, we pass another Victorian fort, this time converted

into holiday accommodation. The beacons alongside it, together with the one on Watwick Point, provide a series of navigation aids to tankers entering Milford Haven. The cliffs nearby are some of the highest on the peninsula and provide excellent views across the mouth of the haven towards West Angle Bay.

Before reaching St Ann's Head at the tip of the peninsula, our route also takes us past the pebbly cove of Mill Bay, where the exiled Henry Tudor landed in 1485 at the start of his successful campaign to seize the English throne from Richard III.

After rounding the headland, easy clifftop walking leads us along the peninsula's windswept western coast to Westdale Bay, a picturesque sandy beach popular with surfers. We are now at the western end of the shallow glacial valley running across the neck of the peninsula. A short level stroll along this valley takes us back to our starting point in Dale.

DALE PENINSULA

DISTANCE: 10.9KM/6.8MILES » **TOTAL ASCENT:** 311M/1,020FT » **START GR:** SM 811058 » **TIME:** ALLOW 3.5 HOURS » **SATNAV:** SA62 3RA » **MAP:** OS EXPLORER OL36, SOUTH PEMBROKESHIRE, 1:25,000 » **REFRESHMENTS:** THE GRIFFIN INN AND THE MOORINGS COFFEE SHOP, RESTAURANT AND BAR, DALE » **NAVIGATION:** EASY AND WELL MARKED.

Directions – Dale Peninsula

➊ Leave the car park via the main entrance and **turn right**. Follow the seafront into the village of Dale and past the the Griffin Inn. Where the road turns sharp right, **keep ahead** on to a lane signed to the Field Studies Centre. This climbs through woods to reach a more open area with clear coastal views to the left.

2 Shortly after the views open out, **turn right** at a National Trail signpost through a small wooden gate. There are fine views across to the Angle Peninsula (Walk 4) before the path dips into woodland behind the small cove of Castlebeach Bay. Cross a footbridge and climb steps back out of the cove. Continue on an undulating path through a mix of woods and fields to a large concrete tower (Watwick Beacon) at Watwick Point.

3 **Bear right** to continue along the obvious coast path. After about 600m, **turn left** through a gate to pass behind Watwick Bay (access to the beach is possible via a steep path on the left). Climb back on to the cliffs above West Blockhouse Point and cross the access track to the former fort (now holiday accommodation). Continue round the back of Mill Bay, a small pebbly cove where the exiled Henry Tudor landed in 1485.

4 Approaching St Ann's Head, pass **to the left** of chalets on an enclosed path then keep **straight ahead** uphill across an open field. Aim for a green gate in front of a row of cottages and **turn right** immediately in front of it. Walk along the field edge as far as a waymarked gate **on the left** and join the access road to St Ann's Head Lighthouse. Opposite, a signed short detour is possible to the Cobblers Hole Viewpoint.

5 Follow the road **to the right** for about 250m. Just after passing an access road to houses on the right, **turn left** where indicated to continue along the coast path. There are no major ups or downs along this clifftop path, so there are plenty of opportunities for you to enjoy the spectacular coastal scenery. After about 3.5km, the path eventually drops from the cliffs, descending steps into Westdale Bay.

6 Leaving the coast, **turn right** and follow a level path across a large field towards Dale. Join a track **to the right** of Dale Castle then **continue ahead** on to a tarmac lane towards the parish church. Roughly 350m after the church, **turn right** on to a track marked with a no-entry sign. This is the alternative exit to the car park (avoiding the one-way system) and will shortly return you to your starting point. If there is a locked gate across the alternative car park exit, continue along the road to a T-junction and **turn right**.

06 DALE PENINSULA

LOOKING EAST ALONG THE COAST FROM NEAR WEST HOOK FARM

07 St Brides & the Marloes Peninsula

Island views along Pembrokeshire's Atlantic coast.

St Brides » Musselwick Sands » Martin's Haven » Wooltack Point » Marloes Sands » Marloes » St Brides

Start

Free national park car park at St Brides. GR: SM 802109.

The Walk

There is something magical about the far west of Pembrokeshire and the coastal scenery around Marloes is some of the most spectacular in the national park. Our route begins with a wonderful stretch of coast path, taking us west from St Brides past Musselwick Sands and on to Martin's Haven, the small harbour where in spring and summer visitors embark for Skomer Island.

The view from Wooltack Point, at the far western end of the so-called 'Deer Park', is the next best thing to visiting the island itself. From here the eastern tip of Skomer is little more than a kilometre away, with the smaller Midland Isle being less than half that. The islands are best known for their seabirds and contain internationally important colonies of puffin and Manx shearwater. The surrounding seas are equally rich in wildlife and are one of only three designated marine nature reserves in the UK.

After rounding the headland, open cliffs lead us past Gateholm Island and behind the beautiful Marloes Sands. To the south-west, there are good views of Skokholm Island, slightly lower in the water than its counterpart to the north. Like Skomer, Skokholm is a designated national nature reserve but can only be visited by prior arrangement.

Leaving the coast, we head inland towards Marloes. The main route described bypasses the centre of the village, but it is worth making the detour if only to see the splendid clock tower built as a memorial to the 4th Baron Kensington. The baron was well known locally as the tenant of St Brides Castle, a nineteenth-century baronial-style house now converted into luxury holiday apartments. Field paths between Marloes and St Brides take us directly below the 'castle', which sits on a low hill above the bay.

ST BRIDES & THE MARLOES PENINSULA

DISTANCE: 16.5KM/10.3MILES » **TOTAL ASCENT:** 496M/1,627FT » **START GR:** SM 802109 » **TIME:** ALLOW 5.5 HOURS » **SATNAV:** SA62 3AJ » **MAP:** OS EXPLORER OL36, SOUTH PEMBROKESHIRE, 1:25,000 » **REFRESHMENTS:** THE LOBSTER POT INN AND THE CLOCK HOUSE, MARLOES » **NAVIGATION:** EASY AND WELL MARKED.

75

76

77

Ferry P (Summer)

Wooltack Point

Haven
Point

Martin's
Haven

High Point

Tusker
Rock

Mouse's Haven

Lookout
Station

Crab Stones

Natural
Arch

3 Scribed Stone

West Hook Farm

Natural
Arch

4 Fort

East Ho
Far

Midland Isle
(MARLOES AND ST BRIDES C.)

Caves

Cave

5

Martin's
Haven

46

59

Trehill
Farm

The Anvil

Limpet
Rocks

Renney Slip

Deadman's Bay

51

Black Stones

ure Reserve

Pitting Gales Point

52

The Bench

Mar
Me

Rainy Rock

Fort

Little Castle Bay

Victoria Bay

Watery Bay

Cave

Albion Sands

Gateholm
Stack

Settlement

Cairn

Gateholm Island

07 ST BRIDES & THE MARLOES PENINSULA

Directions – St Brides & the Marloes Peninsula

❶ Walk past St Brides Church towards a gap in a stone wall. Pass through the gap, following a coast path sign for *Martin's Haven*. Continue through a picnic area and along a field edge, the former estate boundary wall to your right. Shortly leave the field and join a clifftop path, the boundary wall now to your left. Follow the cliffs as far as Musselwick Sands (around 3.7km).

2 After descending to an access point behind the beach, the path climbs inland to the left for around 100m. **Ignore** the path continuing ahead and **turn sharply right** to return to the coastal cliffs. Continue along a clear clifftop path for a further 2.9km to reach the small pebbly bay of Martin's Haven.

> For a shorter walk, take the path **continuing ahead** inland from Musselwick. **Turn left** at a road and rejoin the main route on the outskirts of Marloes.

3 Join the road climbing **to the left**, past toilets and the Skomer Marine Nature Reserve office. At the top of the hill, **turn right** through a gate in a wall and climb straight up the grassy slope ahead.

> The circuit around the Deer Park can be omitted by **turning left** immediately after the gate and following the official coast path parallel to the wall. Rejoin the main route at Renney Slip.

4 At the top of the steps, **fork right** towards a white wooden hut (an automatic weather station) on a hill. **Bear slightly left** from the hut and descend towards the cliffs immediately opposite Midland Isle and Skomer. For the best island views, **turn right** and follow the path up to a level grassy platform above Wooltack Point. Retrace your steps and follow the cliffs round to rejoin the official coast path at Renney Slip.

5 The coast path continues across open grassy cliffs towards Gateholm Island. **Bear right** at the end of the large open area to continue alongside a fence. Once past the 'island', the path **bears left**, above the long curve of Marloes Sands.

6 Soon after climbing a short flight of steps, leave the coast path by **turning left** at a footpath sign. Go through a gate and follow a clear grassy path along the right-hand edge of two fields to a T-junction with a track. **Turn right**, passing toilets and a number

of converted farm buildings (the former Marloes Sands youth hostel), and reach a junction with a road. **Turn right.**

7 About 750m after joining the road, and just past Marloes Court on the right, **turn left** into a field at a footpath sign. Follow the right-hand field boundary ahead until you emerge on a road to the left of a pink house. **Turn right** and enter the village of Marloes. Take the first track **on the left** then immediately **turn right** on to another track.

> For The Lobster Pot Inn and The Clock House, continue along the road into the centre of Marloes. To rejoin the main route, take the road opposite The Lobster Pot, past the public toilets and up to a house called The Fold. Join a path **to the left** of the entrance and emerge in a field. **Keep ahead** along the **left-hand** field edge to a junction with a track and **turn right**.

8 The track ends at a house called The Old School. **Keep ahead** through a kissing gate and follow the path along the left-hand edge of two fields. Shortly after entering a third field, with Fopston Farm across the field to the right, cross a stile **on the left** and join a track. **Turn right** and descend to a track junction in a dip. **Turn right.**

9 Take the second signed path **on the left**, just before a junction with a lane. Follow the right-hand edge of four fields, bypassing the old stone stiles via woodland gates **on the right**. Keep **straight ahead** across a track and then the access road to St Brides Castle. Cross a field towards St Brides Church and walk through the churchyard to the car park.

SKOMER ISLAND, VIEWED FROM MARLOES BEACON

08 St Brides & Borough Head

12.1km/7.5miles

Sweeping coastal views around St Brides Bay.

St Brides » Mill Haven » Borough Head » Talbenny Cross » Lower Broadmoor » St Brides

Start

Free national park car park at St Brides. GR: SM 802109.

The Walk

This is the second of two walks from St Brides Haven, a small cove which traditionally provided the only safe landing point along this stretch of St Brides Bay. Nearby is a medieval if much 'Victorianised' church and also a pump house built to provide fresh water for St Brides Castle to the west. The eponymous St Bride was actually an Irish saint, Brigid, hinting at the strong connections between Ireland and this part of Wales during the post-Roman period.

Our walk takes us eastwards along the coast, initially across rose-coloured sandstone cliffs to Mill Haven. The path is then more undulating as far as Brandy Bay, with a number of steep climbs and descents to tackle. As the cliffs level off towards Borough Head there are excellent views across the sweep of St Brides Bay, right out to Ramsey Island off the tip of the St Davids Peninsula.

East of Borough Head the coast is more sheltered and the cliffs are clothed in numerous sessile oaks. Unlike the closely related pedunculate or English oak, sessile oaks possess stalked leaves and stalkless (sessile) acorns and tend to flourish best in the wetter, upland areas of Britain and along the Atlantic coast. The steep cliffs on which they grow here are very ancient, being formed out of Precambrian igneous rocks some 650 million years old.

For the return leg of the walk, we turn inland towards Talbenny and head west along quiet lanes. A lovely section of historic green lane south of Lower Broadmoor farm provides some relief from the hard tarmac surface. Before reaching Lower Broadmoor we pass close to the disused Talbenny airfield. During World War II, RAF planes flew regularly from here to protect Allied convoys in the Atlantic.

ST BRIDES & BOROUGH HEAD

DISTANCE: 12.1KM/7.5MILES » **TOTAL ASCENT:** 369M/1,211FT » **START GR:** SM 802109 » **TIME:** ALLOW 4 HOURS » **SATNAV:** SA62 3AJ » **MAP:** OS EXPLORER OL36, SOUTH PEMBROKESHIRE, 1:25,000 » **REFRESHMENTS:** NONE ON ROUTE » **NAVIGATION:** EASY AND WELL MARKED.

ST BRIDES HAVEN

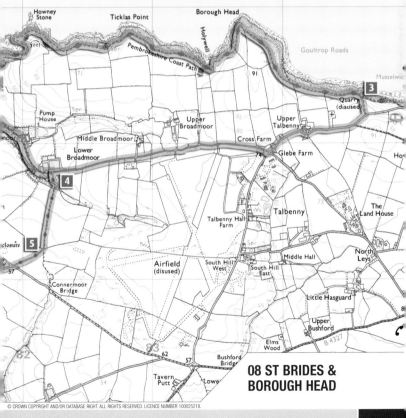

Pembrokeshire Coast National Park/
Parc Cenedlaethol Arfordir Penfro

Howney Stone

Ticklas Point

Borough Head

Goultrop Roads

Musselwic

Fort

Pembrokeshire Coast Path

Holywell

91

3

Quarry (disused)

Pump House

Spr

Upper Broadmoor

Upper Talbenny

Middle Broadmoor

Cross Farm

80

Lower Broadmoor

Glebe Farm

91

4

Ho

The Land House

Talbenny

Talbenny Hall Farm

Talbenny

closure

5

North Leys

57

Airfield (disused)

South Hill West

South Hill East

Middle Hall

Connermoor Bridge

Little Hasguard

Upper Bushford

Elms Wood

B 4327

82

83

62

57

Bushford Bridge

08 ST BRIDES &
BOROUGH HEAD

Tavern Putt

Lowe

54

Directions – St Brides & Borough Head

❺ From the car park, join the track **curving right** towards Cliff Cottage. With the entrance gate ahead, **bear left** towards the sea and drop on to the beach. Cross the small bay and rejoin the coast path **to the left** of the house. With the sea to your left, follow a gently undulating path as far as Mill Haven (around 2.4km), where the path drops to cross a small stream by a wooden footbridge.

> 💠 From Mill Haven, a waymarked path **on the right** leads to Lower Broadmoor farm. On reaching agricultural buildings, keep ahead on to a track and rejoin the main route at the entrance gate to the farm.

2 Between Mill Haven and Brandy Bay the path is steeper and more physically demanding. Continue past Stack Rocks and across open cliffs as far as Borough Head. A short distance beyond the headland, enter an area of coastal woodland (sessile oak). The path later becomes enclosed between hedges.

3 Shortly after the path opens out to the right (St Mary's Church can be seen at the top of the field), **turn right** over a stile and walk up the right-hand edge of a field to a lane. **Turn right**, shortly passing the entrance to the church and then Upper Talbenny farm. At a crossroads just past a group of houses, **turn right** on to a dead-end lane signed to *Broadmoor*.

4 After about 1.6km, reach a gate across the lane marked *Lower Broadmoor Farm* (the point where the shortcut rejoins the main route). Don't go through the gate, but **turn left** on to a track marked *Unsuitable for motors*. This shortly becomes a green lane running between earth banks.

5 At a right-hand bend, join a more defined track in the direction of a barn. Emerge on a tarmac lane to the right of the barn and continue **straight ahead**. After a little under 1.5km, you will reach a left-hand bend by a red telephone box. Keep **straight ahead** on to a lane marked *Unsuitable for buses* (also signed *St Brides*) and follow the narrow shaded road back down to the car park.

ST BRIDGET'S CHURCH, ST BRIDES

SOLVA HARBOUR

09 St Davids to Newgale

A linear walk along the stunning northern reaches of St Brides Bay.

St Davids » Caerfai Bay » Caer Bwdy Bay » Porth y Rhaw » Solva » Dinas Fawr » Porthmynawyd » Newgale

Start

Large pay-and-display car park adjacent to the national park visitor centre in St Davids. GR: SM 757252.

The Walk

The northern curve of St Brides Bay, between St Davids and Newgale, is within easy reach of the main road from Haverfordwest, allowing walkers to access a regular bus service (except on Sundays) and enjoy this fabulous stretch of coastline without compromise. (Timetables can be found on the Traveline Cymru website – see page xi.)

We begin our walk from the national park visitor centre in St Davids (see also Walk 10), from where it is only a short stroll down the lane to Caerfai Bay and the coast path. The sheltered sandy beach here is easily accessible by car and extremely popular with visitors, as is the equally attractive Caer Bwdy Bay a short distance to the east.

After a few miles of varied clifftop walking, we arrive at the entrance to Solva Harbour, one of the most attractive natural harbours in Wales. A classic example of a ria, the harbour was formed when a meltwater valley was partially submerged by rising sea levels at the end of the last ice age. Solva later developed into a major trading hub as well as an important lime-burning centre – four well-preserved kilns can be seen on the beach below the Gribin. There are a number of pubs in the village and it is also possible to catch a bus back to St Davids.

East of Solva, attractive clifftops lead past two jagged peninsulas (Dinas Fawr and Dinas Fach) before a steep descent into the sheltered valley of Porthmynawyd (ablaze with wild flowers during early summer). Returning to the cliffs, we will be able to stretch our eyes along the length of Newgale Sands towards Rickets Head. If the tide is out, we can join the beach at Cwm Mawr and complete our walk into Newgale with a stroll along the sand.

ST DAVIDS TO NEWGALE

DISTANCE: 14.9KM/9.3MILES » **TOTAL ASCENT:** 534M/1,752FT » **START GR:** SM 757252 » **TIME:** ALLOW 5 HOURS » **SATNAV:** SA62 6NW » **MAP:** OS EXPLORER OL35, NORTH PEMBROKESHIRE, 1:25,000 » **REFRESHMENTS:** CAFE ON THE QUAY, HARBOUR INN AND THIRTY FIVE CAFE, SOLVA (PLUS OTHER OPTIONS ON MAIN STREET); SANDS CAFE AND THE DUKE OF EDINBURGH INN, NEWGALE; PLENTY OF CHOICE IN ST DAVIDS » **NAVIGATION:** EASY AND WELL MARKED.

09 ST DAVIDS TO NEWGALE

Directions – St Davids to Newgale

➎ Make your way to the car park entrance (opposite the national park visitor centre) and **turn left** along the road. At the edge of the built-up area, the road **bears left** and descends for around 700m to a car park above Caerfai Bay.

2 Join the coast path at the **left-hand edge** of the car park (signed to *Solva*) and **continue ahead** past two paths on the right leading down to the beach. Follow a fairly level path around a broad promontory then descend steeply into a valley behind Caer Bwdy Bay.

3 **Turn right** after crossing the stream then **fork left** up the hill (**not** the path going down to the beach). Climb back up on to the cliffs and continue along an easy level path past Carreg y Barcud and another small inlet. Approaching Porth y Rhaw, the path swings inland to the left. **Turn sharp right** at a waymarked junction and join a long, stepped descent to the cove.

4 Climb back on to the cliffs to enjoy more fabulous views. About 1.6km after leaving Porth y Rhaw, the path swings inland to the left above Solva Harbour. Go through a gate and follow a field edge to another gate, where you **turn right** (the path ahead continues into Upper Solva). Follow the path down to a house drive and on to a tarmac lane.

5 As the lane swings uphill to the left, **bear right** on to a descending track. After about 30m or so, take the waymarked path down steps **on the right** and descend to the harbour. **Turn left** past Solva Boat Club and follow the harbour edge to a large car park opposite Harbour Inn and the Thirty Five cafe.

  ➲ For a shorter walk, **bear left** to the car park entrance and then **turn right** on to Main Street. The bus back to St Davids stops on the main road outside The Old Pharmacy.

6 Cross a footbridge over the River Solva and **turn left** and then **immediately right** to rejoin the coast path. **Keep right** at a fork to pass above some former limekilns then climb up through trees and out on to the Gribin – a narrow, rocky headland guarding the entrance to Solva Harbour.

7 Drop steeply **to the left** where the path is waymarked to a footbridge in the valley below. Cross a stony beach (Gwadn) and climb up on to the headland on the far side. At the top, **turn sharp left** and shortly join a clear clifftop path. The path now climbs steadily, passing a number of beaches, before cutting across the base of Dinas Fawr – a pronounced rocky promontory jutting out to sea.

> OR There is a narrow path running along the spine of Dinas Fawr which makes for a great scramble if time allows.

8 Beyond Dinas Fawr, you should be able to see Newgale Sands quite clearly. After passing the smaller headland of Dinas Fach, the path swings left to descend into another valley. Cross a small stream at the bottom of the hill and **turn right**. **Do not** continue down to the cove (Porthmynawyd), but **bear left** to climb out of the valley and back on to the cliffs. Follow the path inland again behind Cwm-bach, climbing out of the cove then dropping immediately down into Cwm Mawr.

> OR If the tide is far enough out, it is recommended that you drop down on to the beach and follow it round the headland to Newgale. Where you can see the top of a lifebuoy, leave the beach via a boardwalk across the large stony storm bank. **Turn left** and follow the main road up to the bus stop opposite The Sands cafe.

9 If the tide is high, climb steeply out of Cwm Mawr along the coast path. Descend to the main road and **keep ahead** down the hill towards the village. Buses can be flagged down opposite The Sands cafe (The Duke of Edinburgh can be found a little further along the main road, beyond the bridge).

SOLVA HARBOUR

PORTH CLAIS, WITH CLEGYR-BOIA IN THE DISTANCE

10 St Davids & St Justinian's

15.5km/9.6miles

Heading west in the footsteps of Wales's patron saint.

St Davids » St Non's Bay » Porth Clais » Porthlysgi Bay » Pen Dal-aderyn » St Justinian's » Porth Clais » St Davids

Start

Large pay-and-display car park adjacent to the national park visitor centre in St Davids. GR: SM 757252.

The Walk

This is the second of two walks from the national park visitor centre in St Davids and it explores the wonderful coastal scenery to the west of this historic 'village city' – most of it accessible via fairly level paths. An alternative finish provides a chance to visit the magnificent cathedral.

We begin by following paths down to St Non's Bay, where the eponymous Non is reputed to have given birth to St David in the late fifth or early sixth century. A ruined chapel marks the spot, while close by is a modern chapel and religious retreat built by the Passionists. A short distance to the west is Porth Clais, a small natural harbour with a long connection to St Davids. During the 'Age of Saints' and for many centuries afterwards, pilgrims, disciples and traders would all have used this harbour.

Continuing westward, we pass the stony bay of Porthlysgi before curving north past Wales's most westerly mainland point, Pen Dal-aderyn. To our left, separating the mainland from the humpback ridge of Ramsey Island, are the narrow but often turbulent waters of Ramsey Sound. Ramsey itself is a haven for wildlife and contains the most important grey seal breeding colony in southern Britain.

At St Justinian's there is a lifeboat station and a quay from which summer trips to Ramsey set out. Leaving the coast path, we track back across the peninsula to Porth Clais along quiet lanes. Poking its head above the flat coastal plateau is Clegyr-Boia, a rocky 'island' formed by material from a volcanic eruption over 600 million years ago. These rocks are some of the oldest in Wales and date back to the Precambrian era. A pleasant path from Porth Clais takes us back to St Davids.

ST DAVIDS & ST JUSTINIAN'S

DISTANCE: 15.5KM/9.6MILES » **TOTAL ASCENT:** 372M/1,220FT » **START GR:** SM 757252 » **TIME:** ALLOW 5 HOURS » **SATNAV:** SA62 6NW » **MAP:** OS EXPLORER OL35, NORTH PEMBROKESHIRE, 1:25,000 » **REFRESHMENTS:** PLENTY OF CHOICE IN ST DAVIDS; PORTH CLAIS KIOSK, PORTH CLAIS » **NAVIGATION:** EASY AND WELL MARKED.

**10 ST DAVIDS &
ST JUSTINIAN'S**

Directions – St Davids & St Justinian's

➔ Make your way to the car park entrance (opposite the national park visitor centre) and **turn left** along the road. At the edge of the built-up area where the road bears left, **turn right** into Maes-y-dre. A short distance ahead, where the road bears slightly right, keep **straight ahead** on to an enclosed bridleway behind houses. **Ignore** a path on the left signed to St Non's and the coast path and continue to a junction with a lane.

2 **Turn left** along the lane then take the first footpath **on the right** (just before a sign for *St Non's Chapel and Well*). Follow an enclosed section of path then keep **straight ahead** down the right-hand edge of two fields (in the second field, the ruined St Non's Chapel can be seen to the left). At the bottom of the fields, **bear right** over a stone stile to join the coast path.

3 **Turn right** along a level clifftop path. After a little under 1km, and shortly after passing a National Trust sign, the path **bears right** above the narrow inlet of Porth Clais. At a fork in the path, **keep left** and descend towards the harbour.

4 **Turn left** at the road and then immediately **bear left** again to rejoin the coast path, which climbs above Porth Clais behind some former limekilns. **Keep right** at a fork along the clearer path continuing upwards. With the open sea ahead, go through a kissing gate and reach an immediate fork.

5 Take the path **to the left** and cross open, occasionally exposed cliffs to reach a gate marked *Taid* ('grandfather') near Ogof Lle-sugn. Go through the gate and follow the path round a headland and down on to the stony shore of Porthlysgi Bay. **Turn right** and then **immediately right** again to leave the beach.

6 **Turn left** to follow the coast path up a steep, stepped climb and on to the National Trust property of Lower Treginnis. West of Porth Henllys (where there is a small lake) there are a number of competing paths across the cliffs, but as long as you keep the sea to your left you can't go too far wrong. The paths all come together again at a kissing gate above Ogof Cadno.

7 Soon after the kissing gate, the path **swings right**, level with Ramsey Island, and passes a cairn marking the most westerly point of mainland Wales at Pen Dal-aderyn. There is one short, steep climb from the old quay at Carn ar Wig, but the remainder of the path to St Justinian's is mainly clear and level. In the distance, beyond the lifeboat station, can be seen the distinctive rocky tor of Carn Llidi (see Walk 11).

8 On reaching the lane at St Justinian's, **turn right**. After an initial climb, the road crosses a flat, scrubby coastal plain in the direction of St Davids. A little over 1km after leaving the coast, take the first proper lane **on the right**. Climb past the rocky outcrop of Clegyr-Boia then follow the road **sharply right** and descend to a crossroads. Keep **straight ahead** and follow the lane back down to the coast at Porth Clais.

9 Briefly rejoining your outward route, follow the road across the stream behind the harbour. This time, however, take the path **on the right** immediately past the coast path. After a steep climb, keep **straight ahead** across a field and then along the left-hand edge of a campsite. With the reception block ahead, **turn left** on to the access track and then **immediately right** on to a fenced path along a field edge. Follow an enclosed path to a lane outside the Warpool Court Hotel.

10 Keep **straight ahead** across the lane, rejoining your outward route along the bridleway behind the houses. Follow the path back to Maes-y-dre and keep **straight ahead** to a T-junction. **Turn left** to return to the car park opposite the national park visitor centre.

> **OR** For an alternative finish via St Davids Cathedral, **turn left** by a bin a few metres after rejoining the bridleway. Keep **straight ahead** at a road, which curves right and then sharp left to a T-junction opposite The Boathouse. **Turn left**, past The Farmers Arms, and then **immediately right** into Tower Hill Lane. With the cathedral ahead, follow the lane **to the right** and then **turn left** through a stone arch. After visiting the cathedral and bishop's palace, retrace your steps to the arch and keep **straight ahead** up the hill and through the centre of St Davids. **Fork right** on to a path past the front of the visitor centre to return to the car park.

SECTION 4

North Pembrokeshire Coast

The north coast of Pembrokeshire, facing the Irish Sea, falls into two distinct parts. West of Fishguard, as far as St Davids Head, there is considerable variety of terrain, with a mix of grassy cliffs and small, sheltered bays as well as areas of wilder, more dramatic scenery dominated by rocky coastal hills. Heading east towards Newport, the coast backs directly on to the Preseli Hills and is dominated by the rugged, sloping promontory of Dinas Island. Further north, between Newport and St Dogmaels, tectonic movements have cracked and contorted the cliffs into a series of dramatic geological features creating some of the wildest and most demanding coastal walking in the national park.

WHITESANDS BAY AND RAMSEY ISLAND (ROUTE 11)

11 St Davids Head

A bird's-eye view of the St Davids Peninsula and its rugged northern coast.

Whitesands Bay » Upper Porthmawr » Carn Llidi (181m) » Treleddyd-fawr » Treleidr » Penberry » Penllechwen » St Davids Head » Whitesands Bay

Start

Car park (fee payable) at Whitesands Bay. GR: SM 734271.

The Walk

Viewed from afar, the most striking feature of the St Davids Peninsula's north-facing coast is a line of rocky hills, mountainous in appearance, stretching from Carn Llidi in the west to Carn Penberry in the east. Rising dramatically from the flat coastal plateau to the south, these hills are made of hard igneous rocks formed during volcanic activity some 470 million years ago. More recently, when sea levels were considerably higher than today, the peaks would have formed offshore islands at a time when wave action was busy wearing the peninsula's softer rocks into a level plateau.

From the popular Whitesands Bay, where we begin our walk, we make a beeline for the highest and most westerly of these peaks, Carn Llidi. Climbing to the summit is optional but highly recommended, with views extending across the entire peninsula as well as Ramsey Island. In fine weather,

there is something otherworldly about the quality of the light in this part of Pembrokeshire – a feature noted by numerous artists and poets.

Leaving Carn Llidi, we follow paths along the southern flank of the hills before cutting across the western shoulder of Carn Penberry to the coast. This is a wild, rugged stretch of coastline with cliffs and headlands intersected by a complex patterning of narrow clefts and coves.

From Penllechwen, a rocky ridge extends south-westward to St Davids Head. The surrounding landscape at first appears untouched by human hand but look closer to see it abounds with evidence of past human habitation: the ruined buildings and stone-walled fields of a medieval village, a Neolithic burial chamber (Coetan Arthur), and the ditches and ramparts of an extensive Iron Age fort on St Davids Head itself. A popular stretch of coast path from the headland leads past Porthmelgan and back to Whitesands.

ST DAVIDS HEAD

DISTANCE: 12.1KM/7.5MILES » **TOTAL ASCENT:** 417M/1,368FT » **START GR:** SM 734271 » **TIME:** ALLOW 4 HOURS » **SATNAV:** SA62 6PS » **MAP:** OS EXPLORER OL35, NORTH PEMBROKESHIRE, 1:25,000 » **REFRESHMENTS:** WHITESANDS BEACH CAFE, WHITESANDS BAY » **NAVIGATION:** EASY AND WELL MARKED IN GENERAL, THOUGH FIELD PATHS AND PARTS OF THE COAST PATH MAY NOT BE CLEARLY DEFINED.

All islands in this area are included in
PEMBROKESHIRE / SIR BENFRO

30

72   73   74

Penll

Dar y
Cadno

Porth
Uwch

Gesail-
fawr

FB

Trwyn
-llwyd

Maen
Porth-llong

Porth
llong

Carn Porth-llong

Garnedd
Gwian

Wales Coast Path

Llechenhinen

Ogof Coetan

Carn Llidi

Settlement & Field System

Coetan Arthur
Burial Chamber

Ogof Crisial

Carn Hen

Ogof Golfe
(Caves)

Carn Twlc

Burial
Chambers
Llidi

St Davids Head/
Penmaen Dewi

8
erthios   Cave
Porth-melgan

Porthmelgan

2

Llaethdy

Penlledwen

Upper
Porthmawr

3

Porth-mawr

Craig y Creigwyr

Porth Lleuog

Trwynhwrddyn

Ffynnon
Faiddog

Flynnon
Faiddog

B 4583

Rescue
Station

St Davids
City Golf Club

Whitesands Bay/
Porth Mawr

The Burrows or Tywyn

Mean Low Water

Mean High Water

Pembrokeshire Coast National Park/
Parc Cenedlaethol Arfordir Penfro

11 ST DAVIDS HEAD

Directions – St Davids Head

5 Walk back up the road from the car park, shortly passing some static caravans in a field on the left. Immediately after the caravans, **turn left** on to a dead-end lane climbing towards Carn Llidi. Follow the lane **to the right** then take the next track **on the left**, up towards Upper Porthmawr farmhouse. The track leads up through the buildings and out through a gate on to the open hill. **Keep ahead** to a fork in the right of way.

> **OR** In fine weather, it's definitely worth making the effort to climb Carn Llidi. To do so, **fork left** along the main track then **to the right** by a National Trust sign. The initial climb is along a good-quality track followed by a concrete path. Where the concrete swings right to an old WWII lookout post, keep **straight ahead** on to an unsurfaced path. The final few metres involve a short scramble across bare rock, but apart from that the final pull to the summit is straightforward. Return the same way, **turning sharp left** at the footpath junction above Upper Porthmawr to rejoin the main route.

2 For the main route, take the path **forking right**. After a brief climb, the path **bears right** and continues along the bottom edge of the common. At a junction in a dip, **turn right** through a kissing gate and follow a path downhill to a youth hostel and waymark post.

3 **Turn left** at the post to cross a stile into a field and **continue ahead** along the right-hand edge of fields towards a farm. Cross a track above the farm and continue along the right-hand edge of two more fields. Keep **straight ahead** across a sunken track and **to the left** of an old farm ruin. Maintain direction, joining a left-hand field edge as you approach farm buildings. Go through a gate **to the left** of the farm and on to a track.

> For a shortcut back to the coast, **turn left** up the hill and follow the waymarked path through the line of rocky tors (between Carn-ffald and Carn Treliwyd) and down to the coast at Porth-gwyn. **Turn left** on to the coast path to rejoin the main route.

4 **Turn right** and follow a winding track down through the farm. With Bwthyn-y-Ffald ahead, **turn left** and then **immediately right** in front of Dan-y-Garn. Go through a gate in front of an old-fashioned cottage. **Bear right** and then **turn immediately left** on to an enclosed grassy path leading behind another cottage. Walk through a garden and keep **straight ahead** on to a gravel track leading past more holiday cottages.

5 Where the gravel track ends at Tŷ Uchaf, **continue ahead** on to an enclosed grassy path and then along the right-hand edge of three successive fields. Leave the fields via a wooden gate leading on to a track past farm buildings and cottages. **Keep ahead** along the track, which passes to the left of a lake and then curves right.

6 As you approach the next group of houses and farm buildings, **turn left** at a footpath sign on to an enclosed grassy path. This shortly **bears right** and emerges in a farm. At a junction of gravel tracks, **turn left** and then **immediately right** on to a signed path between cottages. **Swing left** and climb along an enclosed path between hedges, eventually emerging on to open coastal common below Carn Penberry. After a brief descent, reach a junction with the Pembrokeshire Coast Path.

7 **Turn left** and descend steeply. West of Porth y Dwfr (a narrow inlet in the rocks) the path is more level as far as Gesail-fawr and the peninsula of Penllechwen, though no less spectacular for that. After Penllechwen, the path continues along a rocky, heathery ridge stretching south-westwards towards St Davids Head. This part of the trail is not well defined, with walkers tending to make their own route across the open heathland – but it would be difficult to go too far wrong.

8 After rounding the headland, join a clear path leading behind the sandy cove of Porthmelgan. Climb over the next headland and follow the obvious and very popular path back to Whitesands Bay.

12 Trefin, Porthgain & Abercastle 13.2km/8.2miles

Grassy cliffs and rocky coves between Porthgain and Abercastle.

Trefin » Llanrhian » Porthgain » Aber Draw » Carreg Sampson » Trefin

Start

Small free car park in centre of Trefin (off Ffordd yr Afon).
GR: SM 840324.

The Walk

Our starting point, Trefin (or Trevine), is a large hilltop village set slightly back from the coast about halfway between Fishguard and St Davids. Initially we head inland, climbing through fields, before picking up a quiet lane to Llanrhian. From here, a pleasant track and field path lead down to the pretty little village of Porthgain.

This secluded harbour was once a busy industrial port. The main export was stone, used for building roads and quarried in the cliffs nearby. The crushed material was stored in the large brick hoppers that still dominate the one side of the harbour and was loaded directly on to ships via chutes. After a sharp decline during the 1920s, the industry came to an end in 1931.

From Porthgain, there is pleasant coastal walking across grassy cliffs to Aber Draw, a small beach near Trefin. Just above the shore are the remains of a watermill, which closed in 1918 after five centuries of grinding wheat and barley for local villagers. By then, the mill could no longer compete with cheap foreign imports and large, steam-powered mills in towns.

Continuing towards Abercastle, we cross lonely, unspoilt cliffs and pass high above a number of rocky, inaccessible coves. At Pen Castell-coch, the path passes close to the remains of an Iron Age promontory fort. On a fine day, it is worth making a detour along the peninsula to enjoy the splendid coastal views to the south-west.

Abercastle is one of a number of small, pretty harbours to be found in this part of Pembrokeshire. Just west of the village, we climb away from the coast to pass the magnificent Neolithic burial chamber of Carreg Sampson. Continuing past Longhouse to a lane, we turn right and follow the road for a little over a kilometre back to Trefin.

TREFIN, PORTHGAIN & ABERCASTLE

DISTANCE: 13.2KM/8.2MILES » **TOTAL ASCENT:** 413M/1,355FT » **START GR:** SM 840324 » **TIME:** ALLOW 4.5 HOURS » **SATNAV:** SA62 5AU » **MAP:** OS EXPLORER OL35, NORTH PEMBROKESHIRE, 1:25,000 » **REFRESHMENTS:** THE SLOOP INN AND THE SHED, PORTHGAIN; THE SHIP INN, TREFIN » **NAVIGATION:** EASY AND WELL MARKED IN GENERAL; SOME FIELD PATHS MAY BE UNDEFINED.

ABER DRAW, TREFIN

82

Trwyn
Elen

Ynys-fach

Caves

Porth

Cairn   Quarry
(dis)

P

Wks
(dis)

6

Sewage
Works

Coast Path

Porthgain

5

Felindre
House

Henllys

ys Barry
ottages

Llanrhian
Mills

Llanrhian

4

Cemy

Trefacwn

12 TREFIN, PORTHGAIN & ABERCASTLE

Directions – Trefin, Porthgain & Abercastle

❺▸ Leave the car park and **turn left** down the road. At the bottom of the hill, just past Prendergast Caravan Park on the left, **turn right** down a track marked *Pen-yr-Olmarch*. Pass below a house and **keep ahead** on to a woodland path. At a footpath junction in a dip, **turn left** and climb to a stile leading into a field.

2 **Turn left** along the field edge to the corner and then **to the right**. **Turn left** at the next stile and gateway and follow the right-hand edge of a long, narrow field up the hill. Go through a double stile at the top of the field, then **turn left** along the left-hand field edge, still climbing. **Ignore** two gateways in the corner of the field, instead **turning right** along the top edge of the field to a stile and gateway **on the left**. Cut **diagonally right** across the next two fields to reach an awkward stile on to a narrow lane.

3 **Turn left** up the lane to a T-junction with a wider road and **turn right**. Walk along the road for about 1.3km until you reach a junction with another road on the edge of Llanrhian. **Turn left** and walk through the village.

4 At a crossroads in the village, **turn right** for a little under 100m and then **fork right** on to a farm track signed to *Felindre*. Follow the gently descending track until it swings right just below Felindre House. Keep **straight ahead** through a gate and maintain direction to a kissing gate leading into a field. Follow the right-hand edge of the field down towards Porthgain. After leaving the field, pass through a series of kissing gates, **curving right** to cross a stream and emerging on a track.

5 **Bear left** down the track, shortly reaching a junction with a road in Porthgain. **Turn right** and follow the road past the Sloop Inn and down towards the harbour. Join the path **to the right** of the harbour signed to *Abercastell*.

6 You are now on the coast path. Climb to a white obelisk marking the entrance to Porthgain's harbour and **swing right**, towards Trwyn Elen. Pass round Gribinau (a large amphitheatre-shaped bowl in the cliffs) and follow the landward side of a small field. After returning to the cliffs, descend sharply to Pwll Crochan, where a small stream forms a waterfall as it tumbles over the edge of the cliffs.

7 East of Pwll Crochan the path passes through a series of fields. In the third of these, pass **to the right** of a group of standing stones and then **bear right** (below some cottages) to reach a junction with a road. **Turn left** and follow the road down to the small cove of Aber Draw.

> ☞ For a shorter walk, continue up the road into Trefin (you can use a path **on the left** to cut the corner at the bottom of the hill). Walk through the village until you reach a junction by a triangle of grass. **Fork right** (following a sign for *Croesgoch*) then **swing right** into Ffordd yr Afon. The car park is **on the left**, a short distance down the hill.

8 At the bottom of the hill, **turn left** towards the sea along a tarmac path signed to *Abercastell*. With the ruins of Trefin Mill to your left, cross a footbridge **on your right** to continue along the coast path. Climb past a ruined house near Trwyn Llwyd, following the waymark arrow **to the right**. Continue past a number of inaccessible bays – Pwll Olfa, Pwll Llong, Pwll Whiting – before cutting across the narrow neck of Pen Castell-coch.

9 The path now heads east across farmland, shortly passing the tidal island of Ynys Deullyn. As you start to descend towards Abercastle, **turn right** on to a path signed *Carreg Sampson*. Pass **to the right** of a pond and join a concrete track. This climbs up through a field, past the Neolithic burial chamber, and emerges on a lane outside the farm of Longhouse.

10 **Turn left** and follow the lane to a T-junction. Now **turn right** and follow the road for about 1.1km back to Trefin. At a junction of roads round a triangle of grass, **bear left** (signed *Youth Hostel*) and follow Ffordd yr Afon back down to the car park. Alternatively, continue **straight ahead** at the junction to visit the Ship Inn.

13 Aber Bach & Pwll Deri

10.4km/6.5miles

Pebble beaches and a dramatic rocky coastline.

Aber Mawr » Aber Bach » Pwllcrochan » Pwll Deri » Trefasser » Aber Bach » Aber Mawr

Start

Lay-by near end of lane at northern end of Aber Mawr. GR: SM 884348.

The Walk

Our walk begins at the northern end of Aber Mawr – a wide, sandy beach with an impressive storm bank of pebbles. Now a peaceful, secluded spot backed by marsh and woodland, Aber Mawr was once considered by Isambard Brunel as a possible western terminus for his South Wales Railway. What a difference that would have made!

Leaving Aber Mawr, we round the headland to the smaller bay of Aber Bach. Here we walk across an impressive pebbly storm beach, similar to the one at Aber Mawr. An oft-repeated story is that both beaches were created literally overnight during the great Royal Charter Storm of 1859 (named after the *Royal Charter* ship, which sank off the coast of Anglesey), but it is more likely that the storm banks were created gradually, as sea levels rose following the last ice age.

Lovely coastal walking leads us north to Pwllcrochan, a tiny, contorted amphitheatre of a bay cut into softer sedimentary rocks. Access to the pebbly beach is dangerous, but a grassy platform above the bay can be a good place from which to view seals and their pups in the autumn.

Continuing northward, the coastal path climbs on to the great rampart of cliffs forming the southern side of Pwll Deri. The path climbs to a high point of 140 metres, providing great views across the bay towards Strumble Head, and eventually emerges on a lane near a memorial to local Welsh poet Dewi Emrys. At the base of the memorial can be seen the final couplet from his most famous poem, 'Pwllderi'.

The return leg of the walk is simply a case of following quiet country lanes and a farm track back to Aber Bach. An alternative path from the beach leads up to our starting point.

ABER BACH & PWLL DERI

DISTANCE: 10.4KM/6.5MILES » **TOTAL ASCENT:** 363M/1,191FT » **START GR:** SM 884348 » **TIME:** ALLOW 3.5 HOURS » **SATNAV:** SA62 5UX » **MAP:** OS EXPLORER OL35, NORTH PEMBROKESHIRE, 1:25,000 » **REFRESHMENTS:** NONE ON ROUTE; THE CLOSEST PUB FROM THE START IS THE FARMERS ARMS, MATHRY » **NAVIGATION:** EASY AND WELL MARKED.

Directions – Aber Bach & Pwll Deri

➲ From the lay-by, continue down the lane to a turning area at its end. Join the coast path by **turning right** in the direction of a sign for *Pwll Deri*. Follow the coast round to the small bay of Aber Bach and walk across the large stony storm beach.

2 Rejoin the coast path, initially climbing steeply then continuing along an undulating clifftop path. Approaching Pwllcrochan, an attractive but inaccessible bay cut into the cliffs, descend then climb steeply to a waymark post.

> **➲** The footpath continuing inland will bring you out on to a lane at Velindre West. **Turn right** to rejoin the main route.

3 **Bear left** at the waymark post to continue along the coast path. A short, awkward descent is followed by a climb on to the cliffs to the north of Pwllcrochan. Further along, at Penbwchdy, the path climbs on to the line of a rocky ridge – part of a rampart of cliffs stretching all the way to Pwll Deri.

4 From Penbwchdy, the path climbs steadily north-eastward, crossing the occasional patch of bare rock where it is undefined. Beyond Carn Ogof, the walking becomes easier and there is plenty of opportunity to admire the stunning cliffs surrounding Pwll Deri. Emerge on a lane a short distance **to the right** of a memorial stone to the Welsh poet Dewi Emrys.

5 **Turn right** and follow the lane for about 1km to a T-junction. **Turn right** and then **immediately right** again. After a little over 2km, and immediately after passing a road on the left marked *Unsuitable for heavy goods vehicles*, **turn right** through a gateway marked *Treseissyllt*.

6 Follow a gently climbing track past a house and farm buildings. After **bearing left**, the track starts to descend. **Keep left** at a fork and drop to a junction of tracks in a wooded valley. **Turn right** and follow a track in front of a house and down towards the sea. Rejoin the coast path at Aber Bach and **turn left**, back across the beach. This time, take the path **on the left** – marked *Alternative Route* – immediately after leaving the beach. Emerge on a lane and **turn right** to return to the lay-by.

13 ABER BACH & PWLL DERI

LOOKING SOUTH-WEST TOWARDS PENBWCHDY FROM GARN FAWR

14 **Pen Caer**

20.8km/12.9miles

A demanding circuit around the wild Pen Caer peninsula.

Harbour Village » Llanwnda » Pontiago » Garn Fechan » Garn Fawr (213m) » Pwll Deri » Strumble Head » Carregwastad Point » Harbour Village

Start

Free car park in Harbour Village area of Goodwick (signed to left near top of New Hill). GR: SM 947388.

The Walk

Like much of the north Pembrokeshire coast, the Pen Caer peninsula owes its wild and dramatic landscape to events in the Ordovician period, some 470 million years ago. At that time, it lay at the bottom of a southern hemisphere ocean on the edge of two tectonic plates and was the scene of considerable volcanic activity. The hard igneous rocks that formed were highly resistant to erosion and later evolved into the rocky crags – the various 'garns' – that provide the backdrop to this walk.

From Harbour Village, we initially trace the line of rocky crags across the base of the peninsula to Pwll Deri. The highlight of this inland stretch of the walk (parts of which may be wet and muddy) is the ascent of Garn Fawr, the highest and most westerly of the crags. There are extensive panoramic views from the summit as well as more immediate interest in the remains of an Iron Age stone fortress.

After a steep descent to Pwll Deri (see Walk 13), we join the tough, undulating but incredibly beautiful coast path to Strumble Head. As the path approaches the lighthouse, built in 1908 to protect the ferry service between Fishguard and Rosslare, it winds its way through hillocks of volcanic rock, worn smooth by glacial action during the last ice age.

Beyond Strumble Head, there is no let up in the beauty or demanding nature of the path. At Carregwastad Point, we pass close to Carreg Goffa, a stone commemorating an ill-planned invasion by 1,400 French troops in 1797, before unexpectedly plunging into the lushly wooded valley of Cwm Felin – one of the few sheltered spots on the peninsula where trees grow in abundance. After a long day's hike, we eventually swing right, above Fishguard Harbour and back to Harbour Village.

PEN CAER

DISTANCE: 20.8KM/12.9MILES » **TOTAL ASCENT:** 719M/2,359FT » **START GR:** SM 947388 » **TIME:** ALLOW 7 HOURS » **SATNAV:** SA64 0DY » **MAP:** OS EXPLORER OL35, NORTH PEMBROKESHIRE, 1:25,000 » **REFRESHMENTS:** NONE ON ROUTE BUT THE HOPE & ANCHOR INN CAN BE FOUND AT THE BOTTOM OF NEW HILL IN GOODWICK » **NAVIGATION:** GENERALLY EASY AND WELL MARKED.

14 PEN CAER

Directions – Pen Caer

➊ Leave the car park and **turn right** on to a lane. At the first junction, follow the main lane round **to the right** – there are signs for *Tir Fynhad* and *Sibrwd y Môr*. The lane shortly becomes a pleasant track offering wonderful sea views across Fishguard Bay.

2 The track ends in a grassy area by a house. Take the footpath continuing **straight ahead** across a field then climb through scrub to a ladder stile. Continue along an enclosed path, which may be overgrown in places and crosses some muddy tracks used by livestock. Emerge on a lane outside Ciliau Farm.

3 **Keep ahead** to a right-hand bend in the lane then **ahead again** through a gate on to a footpath. Enter a garden, passing to the left of a house, then **bear left** between overgrown walls to a stile. Shortly reach a stepped stone stile in a low wall and emerge in a field. Follow waymarks through fields and rejoin an enclosed path between hedges. Where the path swings left into a field, **turn right** and follow the edge of three fields to Llanwnda. Pass between houses and **keep ahead** to a junction of lanes and tracks.

> **◎** For a much shorter route, take the footpath signed down the lane **to the right** in Llanwnda past St Gwyndaf's Church. The lane shortly becomes a track. **Turn left** at a signpost for *Carregwastad* and follow the waymarked path down to a junction with the coast path in Cwm Felin. **Turn right** to rejoin the main route.

4 Keep **straight ahead** on to a lane marked *Unsuitable for motors*. After the lane turns into a track, **fork left** on to a narrow enclosed track **to the left** of a gate and field. The track climbs steadily then levels off. Cross **straight over** a lane to continue along an enclosed track. Emerge in a field and keep ahead along its right-hand edge to a gate on to a lane.

5 **Bear right** on to the lane, effectively continuing **straight ahead**. Follow the lane round a left-hand bend by houses then take a gravel access track **forking right**. **Keep right** where the track forks and shortly pass to the right of a house called Garn Folch. Continue on to a narrower, grassy track which emerges on to an area of open common.

STRUMBLE HEAD FROM GARN FAWR

6 Bear left at a fork to continue along the bottom edge of the common. After passing through a gate, follow a fence sharply left and then sharply right. Where the path starts to bear slightly right downhill, away from the fence, **turn left** over a rough stone stile and follow a footpath **bearing right**. Climb past the right-hand side of Garn Fechan then drop to a lane opposite a car park.

7 Cross over into the car park and join a clear grassy path leading up to the summit of Garn Fawr. (The main path passes just to the left of the summit, which can be accessed via an easy scramble up to the right.) A steep descent leads down the western side of the hill to Pwll Deri. As you leave the common, **bear left** at a track and **then right** down a tarmac drive to a junction with a lane.

8 Take the track opposite – to the youth hostel – and **turn right** after a few metres to join the coast path. Descend towards the sea then **bear right** at the bottom of the slope past a path on the left leading out to Dinas Mawr. After passing behind Porth Maenmelyn, the path climbs in a north-westerly direction towards Pen Brush before heading north-east towards Strumble Head. There are occasional places where the line of the path is unclear due to wet ground or bare rock, but you can't go too far wrong and there are plenty of opportunities to enjoy this beautiful stretch of coastline.

LOOKING EAST TOWARDS PENRHYN AND THE DISTANT PRESELI HILLS

9 You will eventually emerge in a car park at Strumble Head. Follow the road **to the right**. Just past another parking area, **fork left** off the road on to the continuation of the coast path. Views shortly open up along Pembrokeshire's north coast.

10 The path tracks to the right and then left around the little rocky cove of Porthsychan. A bit further east, at Penrhyn, you will pass an isolated white cottage adjacent to the coast path. Continuing eastward, keep an eye out for Carreg Goffa, the memorial stone at Carregwastad Point erected to commemorate the 'landing of the French' in 1797. Rather unexpectedly, the path then descends into the lushly wooded valley of Cwm Felin.

11 Cross a stream in the valley and climb steeply, passing a path from Llanwnda (the shortcut) as you near the top of the hill. As you approach Pen Anglas, where an obelisk and concrete hut mark the entrance to Fishguard Harbour, the path **bears right**, cutting off the peninsula. **Keep right** at a grassy fork then take a **left turn** at a path junction – look out for the distinctive National Trail acorn symbol if in doubt.

12 Eventually, the waymarked path **turns right** through a gate and climbs along a gravel path up to Harbour Village. Emerge on a road and **continue ahead**. Shortly after the pavement ends, **turn right** up a lane opposite Landscape Cottage to return to the start.

LOOKING BACK INTO PWLLGWAELOD

15 **Dinas Island & Mynydd Dinas**   17.3km/10.7miles

Hills, coast and woodland around the spectacular Dinas Island.

Pwllgwaelod » Aber Bach » Dinas Cross » Mynydd Dinas (307m) » Aber Fforest » Cwm-yr-Eglwys » Dinas Head (142m) » Pwllgwaelod

Start
Free car park close to beach at Pwllgwae-lod. GR: SN 005399.

The Walk
Between Fishguard and Newport, the Pembrokeshire coast backs directly on to the Preseli Hills allowing walks combining coast and hill. The present walk begins at Pwllgwaelod, at the western end of the flat, marshy valley separating the 'mainland' from the rugged, sloping peninsula of Dinas Island. This sheltered valley, much of it now clothed in woodland, was formed near the end of the last ice age by melt-water from a glacier in Newport Bay.

Initially, we head west along the coast path, past the delightful little cove of Pwll Gwylog and on to the sheltered inlet of Aber Bach. Here we follow paths inland, crossing the A487 road and climbing on to the western slopes of Mynydd Dinas. Rounding the hill's southern flanks, there are good views across the woods of Cwm Gwaun and into the heart of the Preseli Hills.

On a fine day, the views from the summit of Mynydd Dinas are fabulous and include a bird's-eye view of Dinas Island below. It's then back to the coast, with a long descent to the peaceful little cove of Aber Fforest. In the woods behind the beach is a lovely little waterfall, also visited in Walk 16.

We now head back to Dinas Island, reaching its sheltered eastern end at Cwm-yr-Eglwys. Protected from prevailing westerlies, this beautiful spot has a calm, tranquil atmosphere and an almost Mediterranean feel, but was still hit hard by the great Royal Charter Storm of 1859 during which St Brynach's Church was destroyed.

The path out to Dinas Head involves a long climb above spectacular cliffs. As we approach the high point there are fabulous views to be had in all directions, including back towards Mynydd Dinas. A long descent winds down the western side of the headland and back to Pwllgwaelod.

DINAS ISLAND & MYNYDD DINAS

DISTANCE: 17.3KM/10.7MILES » **TOTAL ASCENT:** 667M/2,188FT » **START GR:** SN 005399 » **TIME:** ALLOW 5.5 HOURS » **SATNAV:** SA42 0SE » **MAP:** OS EXPLORER OL35, NORTH PEMBROKESHIRE, 1:25,000 » **REFRESHMENTS:** THE OLD SAILOR, PWLLGWAELOD » **NAVIGATION:** EASY AND WELL MARKED ALONG THE COAST; INDISTINCT PATHS ON DESCENT FROM MYNYDD DINAS.

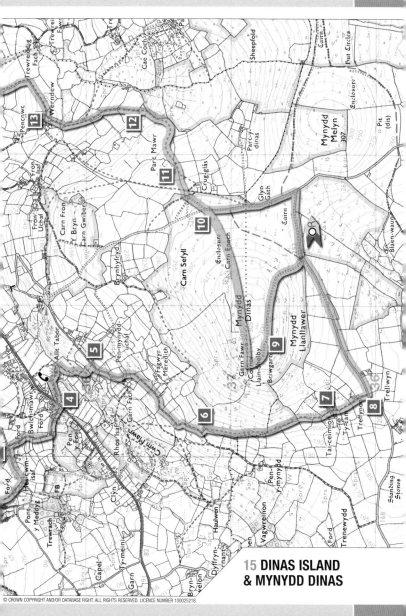

15 DINAS ISLAND & MYNYDD DINAS

Directions – Dinas Island & Mynydd Dinas

6 From the car park entrance, **bear left** towards steps and a coast path sign for *Fishguard*. At the top of the steps, go through a gate into a field and continue along a clear and gently undulating clifftop path. Descend to a footbridge behind a cove (Pwll Gwylog) then climb back up on to the cliffs. Continue along the coast path as far as the pebbly beach at Aber Bach.

2 **Turn left** on to a narrow, stony footpath signed to *Felin Hesgwm*. Emerge on a track by cottages and keep **straight ahead** past Felin Hescwm Refuge to reach a T-junction with a narrow lane. **Turn left** and climb past a house and waterworks building to a signed bridleway on the right.

3 **Turn right** on to the track and pass directly above the waterworks building. Ford a stream (possible wet feet after rain) and climb to a junction of paths. **Bear left** to continue along the bridleway, which now runs on a level across the slope. Join a track by houses and keep **straight ahead** to a junction with the A487 road.

CWM-YR-EGLWYS

4 Cross **straight over** the road to a driveway climbing into Castle Farm Holiday Park. At a house at the end of the drive, **bear right** through a metal gate and then immediately **turn left** on to a grassy path leading to a footpath junction below trees. Take the path **on the right** towards a small metal gate, then climb **diagonally right** across a steep, bracken-covered slope along a narrow, possibly overgrown path. Eventually the path **bears left**, straight up the slope, and reaches a stile and gate leading on to a lane.

5 **Turn right**, past Garn Fach, and on to a farm access track. Where the track turns left through a gate marked *Fagwyr Meredith*, keep **straight ahead** through a gate/stile on to a grassy track marked as a footpath. **Keep right** at a signed junction (effectively **straight ahead**) on to a narrower path heading slightly downhill then contouring across the slope. **Bear left** at the next signed junction, then cross a stile to continue along the bottom edge of a rough field.

6 At far end of the field, **ignore** a path continuing ahead; instead, **bear left**, up the slope, to a stile. Cross the stile and **turn right** to continue contouring across the hill, parallel but slightly above the boundary wall/fence to your right. A muddy area either side of a small stream may require you to detour up the slope for a short distance. After crossing a high, stepped stile set in a bank/wall, follow waymarks across fields to a gap in a hedge.

7 Go through the gap and **turn right**, down the hill, in the direction of a stone ruin. **Turn left** alongside it then continue **straight ahead** across a field in the direction of a house. Go through a gate on to an enclosed grassy track, shortly joining the access track to the house. Keep **straight ahead** to a junction with a lane.

8 **Turn left** and climb gently along the lane, views into the heart of the Preseli Hills to your right. Where the fence ends on your left, **turn left** on to a grassy track heading directly up the hill (**not** sharply back on yourself to the left). The path pulls **slightly left**, in a north-westerly direction, and climbs gently on to Mynydd Dinas.

> In poor visibility, it may be advisable to bypass Mynydd Dinas by continuing along the lane. **Turn left** at a T-junction (signed *Dinas*) and rejoin the main route by a grassy lay-by **on the right** (opposite a grassy path on the left climbing up to Carn Enoch).

9   As the track ahead starts to descend, **bear right** towards the large rocky outcrop of Garn Fawr. **Bear right** again from the rocks, tracking back across the hill in a roughly east-north-easterly direction. As you crest a low brow, you will be able to spot your next target – a rocky outcrop called Carn Enoch. Keep **straight ahead** past this and on to a clear grassy path descending gently north-eastwards to a road.

10   Keep **straight ahead** across the road then **bear slightly left** on to a wide grassy trail. Cross a farm access track and **turn left**, alongside a fence and wall, to reach a stile. Enter a small enclosure and keep **straight ahead** to two stiles in the far corner. Cross the stile **on the right** (effectively **straight ahead**) and descend along the left-hand edge of a large field to a small wooden gate **on the left**.

11   Go through the gate and cross a stile immediately ahead into a field. **Turn right** and follow the field edge down to a corner where the fence turns to the right. **Bear slightly left**, across the middle of the field, and descend to a waymark post in the bottommost corner. Continue down through bracken to pick up a sunken green lane.

12   **Bear left**, either along the lane or through the fields to its immediate left (the top section of the lane is almost permanently wet and boggy). Join the green lane where you can and follow it down to a junction with a stony track. **Bear left** and descend towards two large field gates. Take the one **on the left** and continue down to a farmyard.

13   **Bear right** at the bottom of the yard to join the farm access track and descend gently to a junction with the A487 road. Cross **straight over** to continue down a track opposite signed *To the Coast Path*. As you approach a house, **turn left** through a gate at a footpath sign and follow a waymarked path through a large garden and down into a wooded valley.

14   At a path junction near a waterfall, **bear left** and join a path alongside the stream. Cross stepping stones to the right bank and follow the stream down to the coast at Aber Fforest. **Turn left** on to the coast path and begin a long climb out of the cove. Follow the clear path ahead to a T-junction with a lane.

15 **Turn right** and descend into Cwm-yr-Eglwys. At a junction in the village, **turn right** towards the remains of the former church and then **turn left** on to a road marked *Private Road Footpath Only*. A short distance ahead, follow the road **to the right**.

For a quick easy finish to the walk, **turn left** in front of the public toilets in Cwm-yr-Eglwys on to an alternative coast path route signed to *Pwllgwaelod*. Follow a level surfaced path along a pleasant wooded valley separating Dinas Island from the 'mainland'.

16 With a no entry sign ahead, **bear right** on to the waymarked coast path and begin a long stepped climb through trees. Enter the National Trust property of Pen Dinas, where you will encounter a waymark post marked with green and red arrows. There is a choice of routes, but unless the weather is particularly bad it is recommended that you follow the narrow rugged clifftop path (red arrow) **to the right**. The two options merge near a kissing gate a few hundred metres east of the trig point above Dinas Head. **Bear left** from the trig point for a long descent back to Pwllgwaelod.

CARN ENOCH, BY MYNYDD DINAS

PARROG, BY NEWPORT SANDS

16 **Newport & Carn Ingli**

14.5km/9miles

A walk on the 'mountain of angels' above Newport.

Newport » Parrog » Aber Rhigian » Aber Fforest » Bedd Morris » Mynydd Caregog (311m) » Mynydd Carningli (347m) » Newport

Start

Very cheap pay-and-display car park off Long Street, Newport.
GR: SN 057392.

The Walk

This is another great walk combining coast and hills. Highlights include a fine stretch of estuary and coastal walking west of Newport and stunning panoramic views from the rocky crag of Carn Ingli.

Our walk begins in Newport, a fascinating small town founded by a Norman lord around 1197. The arrangement of the town's streets still reflects the grid patterning of the medieval borough, while the stone castle, now a private home, continues to act as the town's main landmark.

Picking up the coast path, we head west through the old port of Parrog and join the cliffs above Newport Bay. We pass the lovely little cove of Aber Rhigian then reach another small peaceful bay, Aber Fforest. Turning inland, we follow a stream up through woods to an attractive waterfall

(also visited in Walk 15) and join a track climbing towards the Preseli Hills.

Our route takes us quickly on to open moorland and past the impressive standing stone, some two metres in height, of Bedd Morris (Morris's grave). The stone may have been in situ for some 4,000 years and possibly indicates the junction of two ancient trackways. In local folklore, it is linked with a notorious highwayman called Morris.

We now head towards Carn Ingli and a dramatic climb through jagged rocks to its summit. As elsewhere along the north Pembrokeshire coast, the hard dolerite rocks that form the crag are volcanic in origin; viewed from below they create a striking profile. Rich in legend, the hill is often associated with St Brynach (its name translates as 'mountain of angels'), while the remains of a hill fort and Bronze Age hut circles indicate much older human activity. Once off the rocks, a clear grassy path takes us straight down the hill and back into Newport.

NEWPORT & CARN INGLI

DISTANCE: 14.5KM/9.0MILES » **TOTAL ASCENT:** 505M/1,657FT » **START GR:** SN 057392 » **TIME:** ALLOW 5 HOURS » **SATNAV:** SA42 0TJ » **MAP:** OS EXPLORER OL35, NORTH PEMBROKESHIRE, 1:25,000 » **REFRESHMENTS:** PLENTY OF CHOICE IN NEWPORT INCLUDING CASTLE INN, THE CANTEEN, BLAS AT FRONLAS AND THE LLWYNGWAIR ARMS; MORAWELON WATERFRONT CAFE BAR & RESTAURANT, PARROG » **NAVIGATION:** POSSIBLE PROBLEMS IN POOR VISIBILITY; START OF DESCENT FROM CARN INGLI IS UNCLEAR AND MAY BE DIFFICULT TO LOCATE.

COAST PATH NEAR PARROG

16 NEWPORT & CARN INGLI

Directions – Newport & Carn Ingli

➲ Leave the car park by the main entrance opposite Tabernacle Chapel and **turn left** down Long Street. Where the road turns sharply right into Maes Morfa, keep **straight ahead** on to a dead-end road marked *No Vehicular Access to Beach*. Continue down to a junction with a gravel path running alongside the Nyfer estuary (part of the Pembrokeshire Coast Path) and **turn left**.

2 Emerge on a road opposite a house called Neverndale and **turn right**. Pass Morawelon Waterfront Cafe Bar & Restaurant and join a path **to the right** of a campsite. With Rock House ahead, join the beach **on the right** and continue along the foreshore (this part of the route may be submerged at high tide; there is a signed detour around the landward side of Rock House if required). Shortly leave the beach to join a path/ lane climbing above it.

3 Where the surfaced path/lane ends, continue on to a path climbing away from the estuary on to the cliffs above Newport Bay. Follow a clear clifftop path to Aber Rhigian and descend on to the beach to cross a stony storm bank. Climb back on to the cliffs and continue to the next cove, Aber Fforest. Descend a flight of steps and join a track leading down to a footbridge over a stream.

> **☺** As you start descending towards Aber Fforest, look out for a path **on the left**. This cuts through to the concrete track climbing out of Cwm Fforest and avoids a potentially muddy section by the stream and waterfall in the woods (also part of Walk 15). **Turn left** to rejoin the main route.

4 **Turn left** just before the footbridge and cross a grassy area, the stream to your right. Continue on to a woodland path, shortly crossing to the opposite bank of the stream via stepping stones. Approach a waterfall and climb to a junction of paths just beyond it. **Turn left**, back towards the stream, then **bear left** again to cross the stream via a concrete slab above the fall. Climb steps up to the corner of a concrete track.

5 Keep **straight ahead** up the track, climbing steadily and shortly passing round a sharp right-hand bend. Continue to a junction with the A487 road and **turn right** in the direction of a lay-by. From here, cross the road to a track signed to *Havard Stables*. Follow the track up to a farmhouse and **turn sharp left** on to a vehicle track marked with a blue arrow. Continue to climb steadily.

6 Where the track bears right, into the grounds of a house, keep **straight ahead** up a narrow stony track (blue bridleway arrow). **Keep left** at an apparent fork (the clearer path) then **straight ahead** at a junction with a track close to a house. Emerge on the open hill and take the clear path continuing **straight ahead**. This becomes a grassy trail **bearing slightly left** across the hill (there are other paths evident on the ground, but this is the most obvious). Emerge on an unfenced mountain road and **turn right**.

7 Reach a parking area on the left opposite the tall standing stone of Bedd Morris. **Turn left** along the left-hand edge of the car park and join a clear grassy path leading across the gentle slopes of Mynydd Caregog. Continue down the far side of the hill along a clear grassy path and join the line of a fence heading eastwards. You will pass to the left of Carn Edward, a large rocky outcrop in the field to the right.

8 Where the fence turns downhill to the right, **bear slightly left** on to a clear grassy path heading towards the rocky top of Carn Ingli. **Keep left** where the path splits, then **bear right**, back towards the left-hand edge of the rocks. A rough path, not visible until close up, winds up through the rocks to the summit.

9 Follow the rough path to the northern end of the summit area then **drop left** to pick up a clear grassy path heading straight down the hill – there is no obvious route off the rocks, so **take care**. Keep **straight ahead** down the grassy path until you reach a rocky outcrop where the path **bears slightly left**. Continue straight down the slope, passing **to the right** of enclosed fields, and reach a gate in the corner of the common behind a house.

10 Go through the gate and join an enclosed track **to the left** of the house. At a lane with houses ahead, **turn left** on to a track. Join a lane by the next group of houses and follow it downhill **to the right**. **Turn right** at a junction to continue downhill. At a T-junction, **bear left** (effectively **straight ahead**) and pass to the left of a church. Once past the church, follow the road round to the left and then **turn right** into Market Street. At a junction with the main road, keep **straight across** on to Long Street to return to the start.

CEIBWR BAY

17 Cemaes Head & Ceibwr Bay

15.1km/9.4miles

High cliffs and dramatic scenery along Pembrokeshire's wild northern coast.

Ceibwr Bay » Pwllygranant » Cemaes Head » Cwm yr Esgyr » Cwm Trewyddel » Ceibwr Bay

Start

Lay-by off lane to west of Ceibwr Bay. GR: SN 108457.

The Walk

A narrow inlet, barely a stone's throw in width, Ceibwr Bay is the only break in a long, forbidding stretch of cliffs between Cemaes Head in the north and Newport to the south. Either side of the bay are spectacular cliffs, folded and contorted in dramatic fashion during tectonic movements some 450 million years ago (the Caledonian orogeny). This is a wild, lonely stretch of coastline, even by north Pembrokeshire standards, and the coastal path is a real roller coaster, plunging and climbing almost continuously as it traces the cliffs' contortions. The reward is some of the wildest and most beautiful coastal scenery in Pembrokeshire.

From Ceibwr Bay, we follow this dramatic coastline north to Cemaes Head, passing the lovely but inaccessible cove of Pwllygranant and climbing to the highest point on the whole of the Pembrokeshire Coast Path – some 175 metres above sea level.

The surrounding coastal scenery is splendid, with wild, jagged rocks, blowholes and caves, and unreachable shingle beaches frequented by breeding seals in autumn.

A nature reserve and Site of Special Scientific Interest, Cemaes Head marks the northernmost point of the Pembrokeshire coast. The cliffs are less spectacular than those to the south, but it is the views on a fine day that take the breath away: across the Teifi estuary to Cardigan Island then along the whole arc of Cardigan Bay to Snowdonia and the Llŷn Peninsula.

Our return route to Ceibwr Bay follows a mixture of field paths and bridle tracks a short distance inland from the coast. There are some good views and the walking is considerably less taxing than on the coast path. A final descent takes us down into the wooded valley of Cwm Trewyddel, a lovely sheltered cwm behind Ceibwr Bay carved out by glacial meltwater at the end of the last ice age.

CEMAES HEAD & CEIBWR BAY

DISTANCE: 15.1KM/9.4MILES » **TOTAL ASCENT:** 691M/2,267FT » **START GR:** SN 108457 » **TIME:** ALLOW 5 HOURS » **SATNAV:** SA43 3BU » **MAP:** OS EXPLORER OL35, NORTH PEMBROKESHIRE, 1:25,000 » **REFRESHMENTS:** PAVILION CAFE AT PENRALLT GARDEN CENTRE NEAR MOYLGROVE » **NAVIGATION:** EASY AND WELL MARKED EXCEPT FOR SOME SECTIONS THROUGH FIELDS.

17 CEMAES HEAD & CEIBWR BAY

Directions – Cemaes Head & Ceibwr Bay

➲ From the lay-by, follow the coast path around the grassy headland at the entrance to Ceibwr Bay and back out on to the lane. Immediately ahead, take the lane **forking left** down to the bay then **turn sharp left** towards the beach. **Turn right** across a slab bridge over a stream.

2 Climb out of the bay to a junction with a bridleway and **turn left** on to a gently ascending track between fences. Pass a former coastguard cottage then **turn left** across the access track to the house. Descend towards the sea and join a tough, undulating clifftop path.

3 After around 2.2km, begin a long, switchback descent towards the pretty cove of Pwllygranant, where a stream tumbles over the cliffs into the sea. A long climb follows to the highest point on the Pembrokeshire Coast Path (175m). As you pass the high point, views open out past Cardigan Island and along the Ceredigion coast.

   ➲ For a shorter route, **turn right** on to a waymarked path just after crossing the footbridge at Pwllygranant. Follow the waymarked path up the valley, **climbing left** where indicated to a junction with a farm track. Rejoin the main route by **turning right**, up towards the farm buildings of Granant-isaf (point 11).

4 At a footpath junction, **ignore** the stile ahead and **turn left** down steps (the continuation of the coast path signed to *Poppit*). Continue along the top of near-vertical cliffs above the pebbly beach of Traeth Godir-coch and through a gate marked *Cemaes Head Nature Reserve*. Follow the clear path out to Cemaes Head at the entrance to the Teifi estuary.

5 Follow the path **to the right**, parallel to the estuary. After leaving the nature reserve, join an enclosed track leading to Allt-y-goed farm. Continue through the yard and up the hill to join a lane. Descend as far as a house drive on the right marked *Vagwrlas*.

6   **Turn right** on to the steep driveway leading up to the house. Pass to **the immediate left** of the house and cross a stile into a field. Keep **straight ahead** up the hill to a gateway and along the right-hand edge of two further fields. Cross a stile **to the left** of a white house and **turn right**, along a field edge to another stile. Emerge on the corner of a lane by a house called Greenfield.

7   Keep **straight ahead** along the lane, which shortly continues as a farm track marked as a public bridleway. At a sharp right-hand bend, keep **straight ahead** through a field gate on to a grassy bridle track. Follow the bridleway downhill to a junction of bridle paths by a ruined chapel and **turn right**.

8   With a metal field gate ahead, cross a stile **on the left** at a footpath sign and drop towards a forestry plantation. Descend **diagonally right** along the waymarked path through the forest and emerge on a farm track. **Bear right** (effectively **straight ahead**).

9   Approaching farm buildings, cross a stile **on the left** on to a signed bridleway. **Turn right** and **then left** to join a grassy sunken lane between drystone walls. Follow the track **to the right** at a corner and go through a gate into woods.

10   Where the bridleway turns sharply to the left, keep **straight ahead** along a footpath. Shortly emerge from the woods and keep **straight ahead** along the top left-hand edge of two fields to reach a stile and gate. Cross a rough track to a double stile in a wide hedge and emerge on a gravel farm track. **Turn left** up the hill towards the farm buildings of Granant-isaf.

11   Follow the track **to the left** at the farm, towards the farmyard, then **turn right** over a stile by gates. Pass **to the right** of a barn and go through a small wooden gate into a field. Keep **straight ahead** along the bottom right-hand edge of the field then cross three closely spaced stiles. **Bear slightly right** in the next field to a stile **then ahead** to a gate leading into a garden. Pass between a shed and cottage and out on to a track.

12 **Turn left** and **then right**, following a bridleway sign along a cobbled track. Where the main track continues through a gateway marked *Foel Hendre*, keep **straight ahead** on to a grassy bridle track between hedges. This eventually emerges on a lane by farm buildings.

13 **Turn right** at the lane and **then immediately left** on to a concrete track marked as a bridleway and signed *Cwm Connell*. In front of holiday cottages, follow the track **sharply left** and **then right** (the surface has now changed to gravel). Climb steadily until you emerge on road.

14 **Turn right** for a short distance until you reach a lay-by and picnic tables on the right. **Turn right**, past the picnic tables, to the start of a footpath signed to the coast path. Descend through a field to a gate and stile in the bottom right-hand corner then **continue ahead** downhill through scrub. Emerge on a surfaced road and **bear left** in front of Penrallt Garden Centre (cafe).

15 Keep **straight ahead** towards a gate signed *Woodland & Coastal Walk*. Follow the waymarked path around the perimeter of the garden centre and down through woods. At a path junction on the valley floor, **turn right** and follow a stream down towards the coast. At a surfaced lane, **bear left** across the stream and shortly emerge back in Ceibwr Bay. Retrace your steps up the hill **to the left** and back round the headland to your parking place.

CEIBWR BAY

SECTION 5

Preseli Hills

The Preseli Hills are an area of upland extending from Mynydd Dinas in the west to Crymych in the east. They can be divided into two distinct parts: a line of smaller hills running parallel to the coast between Mynydd Dinas and Carn Ingli, and the main group of hills – connected by an ancient trackway known as the Golden Road – between Foel Eryr and Foel Drygarn. Separating these two lines of hills is the steep-sided Gwaun Valley – a ribbon of green woodland in an area otherwise characterised by boggy, acidic moorland. Rich in legend, the hills are famous for their prehistoric remains, including numerous Neolithic and Bronze Age cairns and several prominent hill forts.

WOODLAND PATH SOUTH OF LLANERCH

18 **Cwm Gwaun**

11.9km/7.4miles

Discovering Pembrokeshire's 'secret' valley.

Allt Pontfaen » Llanerch » Mynydd Caregog (311m) » Cwm Gwaun » Allt Pontfaen

Start

Free car park (Allt Pontfaen) near Cwm Gwaun. GR: SN 024339.

The Walk

The steep-sided Gwaun Valley cuts through the heart of the Preseli Hills, its densely wooded slopes a stark contrast to the open, bare hills above it. In geological terms, the valley is a recent formation, owing its size and distinctive V-shape to the huge volumes of meltwater that flowed below the retreating glaciers at the end of the last ice age. This walk explores the rich habitat of woods, marshes and water meadows along the valley floor as well as venturing up on to the bare moors above.

We begin at Allt Pontfaen (Pontfaen Wood), a woodland nature reserve near the hamlet of Cwm Gwaun. The reserve itself covers only a relatively small area, but its steep-sided slopes, densely packed with oaks, are typical of the broadleaf woodlands to be found along the length of the Gwaun

Valley. These are at their most attractive in spring when they are filled with the vibrant colour of wild bluebells.

After following woodland paths as far as Llanerch, we climb out of the valley and up on to Carningli Common. Heading west, we cross the broad summit of Mynydd Caregog (where we can enjoy splendid sea views) and emerge on a mountain road by the standing stone of Bedd Morris. This stone, also visited on Walk 16, may have been in situ for some 4,000 years and possibly indicates the junction of two ancient trackways.

Heading back into the Gwaun Valley, we exchange the open moor for fields and then steeply wooded slopes, eventually emerging on a road. A stroll through Cwm Gwaun takes us past the Dyffryn Arms, a real time capsule of a pub known locally as 'Bessie's'. A drink in the front-room bar provides a fantastic insight into past and present life in this 'secret' valley.

CWM GWAUN

DISTANCE: 11.9KM/7.4MILES » **TOTAL ASCENT:** 349M/1,145FT » **START GR:** SN 024339 » **TIME:** ALLOW 4 HOURS » **SATNAV:** SA65 9SF » **MAP:** OS EXPLORER OL35, NORTH PEMBROKESHIRE, 1:25,000 » **REFRESHMENTS:** THE DYFFRYN ARMS, CWM GWAUN » **NAVIGATION:** LOW-LEVEL PATHS ARE WELL MARKED BUT POOR VISIBILITY MAY BE A PROBLEM ON MYNYDD CAREGOG.

MYNYDD CAREGOG

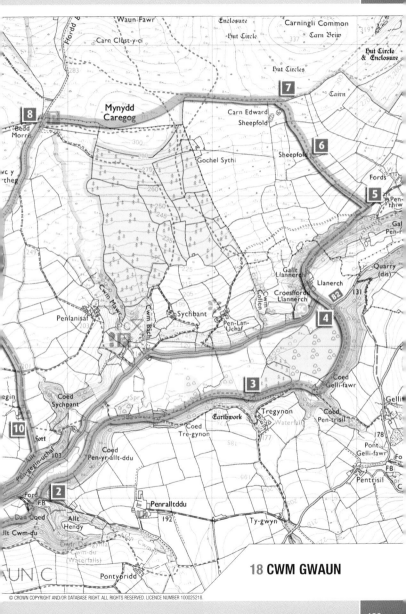

18 CWM GWAUN

Directions – Cwm Gwaun

➊ From the car park, take the footpath into the woods. The path runs along the bottom edge of the trees, close to the valley floor, with fields and the Afon Gwaun visible from time to time on the left. **Keep ahead** past two paths climbing steeply to the right. After the second of these, descend **to the left** and pass behind a farm. **Ignore** a gateway leading on to a rough track and **keep ahead** to a footbridge over a stream. Once over the bridge, join the track and **continue ahead**.

2 Where the track swings uphill to the right, keep **straight ahead** across a stile to join a footpath continuing along the lower edge of the woods. **Ignore** a path leading into fields on the left then another path forking uphill to the right. **Bear left** across a stream, briefly leaving the woods into a more open area. Shortly after re-entering the trees, reach a junction of paths just beyond a bench and wooden gate.

3 Take the path heading downhill **to the left**. After the path levels off, keep **straight ahead**, shortly reaching a river and crossing via a footbridge. On the far bank, **bear left**, away from the river, and use stepping stones to cross a flat marshy area. Climb through woods to a footpath junction and take the unsigned path **continuing ahead** and then slightly **to the left** (the path on the right is signed to *Gellifawr*). Emerge from the woods and reach a junction with a lane.

4 Follow the road **to the left** for about 100m as far as a left-hand bend. Keep **straight ahead** into the grounds of a house called *Llannerch* following a sign for *Dolrannog*. Join a gravel track **to the left** of the house and immediately begin a steep climb through woods. As the track levels off, pass below and **to the right** of a barn and reach a junction of tracks outside Penrhiw Farm.

⊕ For a shorter, low-level route, you can follow the valley road all the way back to Cwm Gwaun, a distance of some 3.7km (2.3 miles).

5 **Turn left** at the entrance to the farm, following a footpath sign up an enclosed sunken track. Enter a field and **keep ahead** up a track climbing along the right-hand edge of the field to a gate and stile. The track then ends, but **keep ahead** up the right-hand edge of two further fields and on to an enclosed grassy track.

6 At the top of the track, cross a stile to the left of an old sheepfold. **Keeping ahead**, climb across a field to a stile in the top fence, a short distance to the right of two rocky outcrops known as Carn Edward. **Bear slightly left** in the next field, just to the right of the outcrops, and climb to a gate and stile leading out on to the open hill.

7 **Turn left** on to a grassy path running alongside the boundary fence. Where the fence turns sharply to the left, strike out across the common, **bearing slightly left** up the gentle slopes of Mynydd Caregog. An equally gentle descent leads to a road and parking area opposite the Bronze Age standing stone known as Bedd Morris.

8 **Turn left** along the road and begin a gentle descent off the mountain. About 200m after passing a track forking left, look for a small bridleway sign on the right-hand side of the road pointing to the left. **Bear left** opposite the sign on to a faint grassy track leading towards two gateways. The right of way goes through the gate **on the left**, then **turns immediately right** through another gate into a field.

9 Descend along the left-hand edge of two fields, **bearing slightly right** at the bottom of the second field to continue along the left-hand edge of a third field. At the bottom of this field, **keep ahead** on to a gravel track enclosed between hedges. Continue past a house, then **bear slightly left** to a gate in a corner to join a sunken, possibly muddy track below trees.

10 Emerge in a field and **keep ahead** down the right-hand edge to a wooden gate leading into woodland. Follow the track **to the right**, initially along the top edge of the trees. After a while, the track steepens then turns round a sharp left-hand bend. Descend to a lane on the valley floor and **turn right**. Follow the road back to Cwm Gwaun. Just past the Dyffryn Arms, **fork left** on to a lane signed to *Pontfaen Church*. Cross the bridge over the Afon Gwaun to return to the car park.

FOEL FRYR PHOTO: TRACY BURTON

19 Foel Cwmcerwyn & Foel Eryr   17.5km/10.9miles

From a former slate quarry to the highest peak in Pembrokeshire.

Rosebush » Foel Cwmcerwyn (536m) » Bwlch Pennant » Foel Eryr (468m) » Tafarn-y-bwlch » Bwlch Pennant » Pantmaenog Forest » Rosebush

Start

Free car park at bottom of lane below Tafarn Sinc. GR: SN 075295.

The Walk

In their heyday, the Rosebush and Bellstone slate quarries on the southern edge of the Preseli Hills employed around 100 men, most of whom lived in the twenty-six cottages of Rosebush Terrace built to house the quarrymen and their families. The quarries have long since closed and Rosebush is now a popular base for outdoor enthusiasts, with the nearby Pantmaenog Forest attracting horse riders and mountain bikers as well as hikers.

Initially, our walk skirts the edge of this forest, climbing steadily across open moor to the summit of Foel Cwmcerwyn (536 metres), the highest point in the national park. In fine weather, views stretch across the full width of Pembrokeshire, from coast to coast, as well as east across Carmarthenshire to the Gower Peninsula and the Brecon Beacons National Park.

Heading north, we join a stretch of the Golden Road, the ancient trackway running along the main spine of the Preseli Hills. This ridge is believed to have been used as a pathway for over 5,000 years, possibly as part of a major trade route linking Ireland and the west of England. Evidence of prehistoric activity can be found on the slopes of Foel Eryr to the west, where there is a stone enclosure complex as well as a Bronze Age burial cairn.

Our route forms a figure of eight, so we can shorten our walk by returning directly to Rosebush from Bwlch Pennant, before or after visiting Foel Eryr. The full route loops around the western and northern slopes of the hill, returning to Bwlch Pennant from Tafarn-y-bwlch along a steadily ascending moorland path. Forestry tracks then provide an easy descent through Pantmaenog Forest and back to Rosebush – along with the chance to enjoy a more sedentary form of pleasure in the wonderful Tafarn Sinc.

FOEL CWMCERWYN & FOEL ERYR

DISTANCE: 17.5KM/10.9MILES » **TOTAL ASCENT:** 603M/1,978FT » **START GR:** SN 075295 » **TIME:** ALLOW 5.5 HOURS » **SATNAV:** SA66 7QU » **MAP:** OS EXPLORER OL35, NORTH PEMBROKESHIRE, 1:25,000 » **REFRESHMENTS:** TAFARN SINC, ROSEBUSH » **NAVIGATION:** POSSIBLE PROBLEMS IN POOR VISIBILITY; INDISTINCT PATHS WEST OF FOEL ERYR.

19 FOEL CWMCERWYN & FOEL ERYR

Directions – Foel Cwmcerwyn & Foel Eryr

❻ Walk up the lane from the car park, past Tafarn Sinc, to the junction with the main lane through Rosebush. Cross **straight over** to a gate and climb up the middle of a field. At the top, go through a gate on to a track and **bear left** into another field. **Turn right** and follow the **right-hand edge** of two fields up to a stile on to a grassy track.

2 **Turn left** on to the track and climb steadily along the edge of Pantmaenog Forest. Cross a boggy section where the forest edge briefly deviates to the left, then continue alongside the fence until you reach a gate where the trees form a corner. **Keep ahead** through the gate and follow a clear path steeply uphill to the summit of Foel Cwmcerwyn.

3 **Keep ahead** from the summit, bearing roughly north at first then slightly west of north. After a gentle descent, cross a level marshy area towards a fence **on the left** and follow this to a kissing gate in a corner. **Turn left** after the gate and descend alongside the fence to another corner. **Turn left** again, continuing to handrail the fence, then go through a gate **on the left** to join a track. Maintain direction, now with the fence to your right, and shortly reach a signed junction at Bwlch Pennant.

　　◉ For a shorter route, take the track **to the left** signed to *Rosebush* (point 11).

4 Go through the gate **on the right** and **turn left**. Because of marshy ground there is no clear path initially, but you need to cut **diagonally right** towards the next fence corner along the forest boundary. After rejoining the line of the fence, the path is drier and more defined. Drop gently to a gravel parking area alongside the B4329.

5 Cross the road and follow a grassy path **to the left**. After about 50m or so, **bear right** and climb steeply to the summit of Foel Eryr.

　　◉ The walk can be shortened from Foel Eryr by retracing your steps to Bwlch Pennant and **turning right** (point 11).

6 **Continue ahead** from the summit, descending steeply down the mountain's western slopes. Before long, you should pick up a fairly well-defined path. Where you reach a footpath sign pointing left, **turn right** on to a narrow, contouring trod. At another waymark post, **bear left** and descend across a wet marshy area with no clear path. Pick your way across wet ground then drop to a fence above a farm.

7 **Bear right** and descend alongside the fence towards the farm. **Do not** enter the farmyard, but **keep right** of the buildings across open moorland. Continue downwards, passing **to the right** of a former quarry, and join a rutted track. Descend **to the left** of another farm, then **to the right** of a cottage, and emerge on a road.

8 **Turn right** and follow the lane for about 800m. As the road descends into a dip, **turn right** on to a track signed to *Tafarn Bwlch*. You will immediately reach a ford with a footbridge to the right. Climb past a stone cottage and **continue ahead** through a waymarked gate. After a steady climb, **curve left** into the yard of another cottage.

9 Cross a stream after the house and **bear left** through a gate. Follow the waymarked track uphill through trees. Where the gravel track bears left into a field, keep **straight ahead** up a green lane. Emerge in a field and **turn right**. Climb steadily along the bottom edge of the field, then **keep ahead** on to a defined track. This becomes enclosed and climbs to a farm

10 Pass through the farmyard then immediately **turn right** on to a gravel track. Cross open moorland to a T-junction and **turn right** on to an unfenced road (the B4329). After a little over 300m, **fork left** on to a gravel track. The surfaced track ends after a few metres, but continue climbing along a faint grassy track towards Bwlch Pennant.

11 Cross your outward route at the top of the hill, keeping **straight ahead** through a gate on to a track signed *Rosebush*. Descend to join another track, **bearing slightly right** at the junction. Where the main track bears left past a sign marked *Private*, take a smaller track **forking right** and continuing downhill.

12 At a junction with a wider gravel track, **turn right** to continue down the valley. **Keep ahead** through a gate and barrier (**ignore** a track to the right) and pass the former Bellstone and Rosebush quarries. Join a lane past a row of terraced cottages, then **turn right** by the Old Post Office to return to the car park.

20 Mynachlog-ddu & Foel Drygarn   15km/9.3miles

Ancient stones and a 'golden road' in the heart of the Preseli Hills.

Mynachlog-ddu » Beddarthur » Carn Menyn (365m) » Foel Drygarn (363m) » Mynachlog-ddu

Start

Gravel parking area (Bethel car park) in Mynachlog-ddu, just to the north of Bethel Chapel. GR: SN 145304.

The Walk

Among Welsh speakers, Mynachlog-ddu is best known for its connections with the poet Waldo Williams (1904–1971), who spent four formative years of his childhood in the village. This walk explores the same line of hills that inspired the poet and takes in some of their most important prehistoric sites.

Heading west from Mynachlog-ddu, we pass a memorial to Waldo, then leave the road to climb along a grassy bridle track leading up to the Golden Road, the ancient trackway running along the main spine of the Preseli range.

Turning eastward, we climb to Carn Bica, an impressive outcrop overlooking Beddarthur ('Arthur's Grave'): sixteen small stones in the shape of a horseshoe. It is not clear what their function was or when exactly they were placed here, but like many other prehistoric remains in the

Preseli Hills they have come to be linked with the legend of King Arthur.

Continuing along the ridgeline, we detour from the main track to take in the craggy outcrops of Carn Menyn. Traditionally, these were believed to be the source for the bluestone used to build Stonehenge, but more recent geological evidence suggests a site of origin further north. Whether it was people or glaciers that transported the four-ton megaliths to Salisbury Plain remains an open question.

Foel Drygarn is the most easterly of the main line of hills, lying just to the north of the Golden Road. The summit is a historical palimpsest, consisting of an extensive Iron Age complex built around three large Bronze Age burial cairns. There are fantastic views in all directions.

Once off the hill, an old green lane (boggy in places) takes us south across the valley towards Foel Dyrch. Here we join a quiet road for the final few kilometres back to Mynachlog-ddu.

MYNACHLOG-DDU & FOEL DRYGARN

DISTANCE: 15KM/9.3MILES » **TOTAL ASCENT:** 354M/1,161FT » **START GR:** SN 145304 » **TIME:** ALLOW 5 HOURS » **SATNAV:** SA66 7RX » **MAP:** OS EXPLORER OL35, NORTH PEMBROKESHIRE, 1:25,000 » **REFRESHMENTS:** NONE ON ROUTE; THE NEAREST PUB IS THE CRYMYCH ARMS INN, CRYMYCH » **NAVIGATION:** FAIRLY EASY IN GOOD WEATHER BUT CAN BE AFFECTED BY POOR VISIBILITY.

20 MYNACHLOG-DDU & FOEL DRYGARN

Directions – Mynachlog-ddu & Foel Drygarn

➐ From the car park, **turn right** and follow the road into the centre of the village. **Turn left** at a T-junction and walk through the village until you reach a lane **on the right** signed to *Rosebush* and *Cofeb Waldo*. Join this lane and climb gently to a cattle grid leading on to open common.

2 Follow the lane **to the left**, across the common, passing a memorial to the Welsh poet Waldo Williams and a bluestone pillar marking the site of origin of the Stonehenge menhirs. Go round a right-hand bend and climb between fences.

3 Where the common opens out again, **do not** follow the road to the left, but keep **straight ahead** on to a grassy bridleway climbing **diagonally left** across the slope of the hill (**ignore** a path turning immediately right straight up the hill). At an obvious fork, **keep right** to continue climbing (**not** the path descending into the valley on your left). The path disappears in an area of wet, marshy ground, but aim for a saddle in the line of hills ahead and you should soon pick up a clear path again.

4 On reaching the saddle, **turn right**, climbing initially then levelling off in the direction of Carn Bica. Pass **to the right** of the outcrop then descend past Beddarthur – sixteen small stones arranged in the shape of a horseshoe – and down a clear grassy path into a saddle below Carn Menyn. Cross a marshy section near the bottom of the slope then join a clear path climbing **to the left** of Carn Menyn. **Fork right** towards the group of craggy outcrops forming the high point of the ridge.

5 Follow the line of rocks **to the left**, slowly bearing back round to return to the main bridleway along the ridge. **Bear right** and continue towards the left-hand edge of a forestry plantation. The track then continues along the edge of the plantation with the trees to your right. At the far end, **turn left** on to a path leading up to the summit of Foel Drygarn.

> **☞** To avoid the additional ascent of Foel Drygarn, **continue ahead** along the main bridle track, following the fence on your right down to the bottom corner of the common to rejoin the main route.

6 From the summit area, **turn right** to pick up a path descending down the south-east slope of the hill. The path continues down a gentle slope to a bridle gate in the corner of the common. Go through the gate and take the track **forking left** opposite an information board. Follow the track round a sharp right-hand bend and then a left-hand bend to reach a junction with a road.

7 Keep **straight ahead** across the road to a wooden field gate leading on to a grassy bridleway between fences. Where the common opens out, **bear right** in the direction of a field gate and beyond this a large television mast on a hill. Join an enclosed bridle track **to the right** of the gate and climb steadily, **ignoring** paths to the left or right. After leaving the fields, continue across an area of rough, marshy moorland until you reach a gate leading on to the corner of a lane.

8 **Turn right** and follow this quiet road for around 3.2km until you reach a T-junction on the edge of Mynachlog-ddu. **Turn right** again to return to the start.

COASTAL VIEWS NEAR CARN MENYN PHOTO: TRACY BURTON

Appendix

The following is a list of Tourist Information Centres, shops, cafes, pubs, websites and other contacts that might come in handy.

Tourist Information Centres

www.visitpembrokeshire.com – official website for Pembrokeshire tourism.
www.pembrokeshirecoast.wales – website for the Pembrokeshire Coast National Park.

Cardigan	T: 01239 613 230
Fishguard	T: 01437 776 636
Haverfordwest	T: 01437 763 110
St Davids	T: 01437 720 392
Tenby	T: 01437 775 603

Food and Drink
Cafes
(The list below is not exhaustive; see individual routes for recommendations.)

The Bothy Tea Room Colby Woodland Garden	T: 01834 814 163
The Pirate Restaurant Amroth	T: 01834 812 757
Ye Olde Worlde Cafe Bosherston	T: 01646 661 216
The Boathouse Tearoom Stackpole Quay	T: 01646 672 687
Wavecrest Cafe West Angle Bay	T: 01646 641 457
Cookhouse Cafe Chapel Bay Fort	T: 07437 568 654

PENTRE IFAN BURIAL CHAMBER, NEAR NEWPORT

Quayside
Lawrenny Quay   T: 01646 651 574
The Clock House Cafe
Marloes   T: 01646 636 527
The Cafe on the Quay
Solva   T: 01437 721 725
The Thirty Five Cafe
Solva   T: 01437 729 236
The Sands Cafe
Newgale   T: 01437 729 222
Porth Clais Kiosk
Porth Clais   T: N/A
Whitesands Beach Cafe
Whitesands Bay   T: 01437 720 168
The Shed Bistro
Porthgain   T: 01348 831 518
The Canteen
Newport   T: 01239 820 131
Blas at Fronlas
Newport   T: 01239 820 065
Morawelon Cafe Bar & Restaurant
Parrog   T: 01239 820 565
Pavilion Cafe
Penrallt Garden Centre   T: 01239 881 295

Pubs

(The list below is not exhaustive; see individual routes for recommendations.)

The Amroth Arms
Amroth   T: 01834 812 480
The Smugglers Bar
Amroth   T: 01834 812 100
The Wisemans Bridge Inn
Wisemans Bridge   T: 01834 813 236
St Govan's Inn
Bosherston   T: 01646 661 311

The Old Point House
Angle   T: 01646 641 205
The Hibernia Inn
Angle   T: 01646 641 517
The Lawrenny Arms
Lawrenny Quay   T: 01646 651 367
The Griffin Inn
Dale   T: 01646 636 227
The Lobster Pot Inn
Marloes   T: 01646 636 233
The Harbour Inn
Solva   T: 01437 720 013
The Duke of Edinburgh Inn
Newgale   T: 01437 720 586
The Sloop Inn
Porthgain   T: 01348 831 449
The Ship Inn
Trefin   T: 01348 831 445
The Farmers Arms
Mathry   T: 01348 831 284
The Hope & Anchor Inn
Goodwick   T: 07754 677 150
The Old Sailors
Pwllgwaelod   T: 01348 811 491
Castle Inn
Newport   T: 01239 820 742
The Llwyngwair Arms
Newport   T: 01239 821 554
Dyffryn Arms
Cwm Gwaun   T: N/A
Tafarn Sinc
Rosebush   T: 01437 532 214
The Crymych Arms Inn
Crymych   T: 01239 831 435

Accommodation
Youth Hostels

YHA Youth Hostels can be found in the following places. For more information please visit:
www.yha.org.uk

Broad Haven	T: 0345 371 9008
Manorbier	T: 0345 371 9031
Newport	T: 0345 371 9543
Poppit Sands	T: 0345 371 9037
Pwll Deri	T: 0345 371 9536
St Davids	T: 0345 371 9141

Hotels, B&Bs and Self-catering

www.visitpembrokeshire.com/
holiday-accommodation
For further information, contact a Tourist Information Centre in the area in which you intend to stay.

Camping

www.camping-wales.co.uk
Provides a good overview of the campsites available in the Pembrokeshire Coast National Park. For more information, contact a local Tourist Information Centre.

Weather

www.metoffice.gov.uk
Provides a seven-day weather forecast for places in the national park.

Outdoor Shops

Morris Brothers, Tenby
T: **01834 842 105/01834 844 789**
www.morris-brothers.co.uk

Mountain Warehouse
Haverfordwest   T: **01437 776 713**
www.mountainwarehouse.com

Mountain Warehouse
Tenby   T: **01834 844 432**
www.mountainwarehouse.com

Outdoor Life
Haverfordwest   T: **01437 763 770**

Other Publications

Day Walks in the Brecon Beacons
Harri Roberts, Vertebrate Publishing –
www.v-publishing.co.uk

Day Walks in Snowdonia
Tom Hutton, Vertebrate Publishing –
www.v-publishing.co.uk

Wales Mountain Biking/Beicio Mynydd Cymru
Tom Hutton, Vertebrate Publishing –
www.v-publishing.co.uk

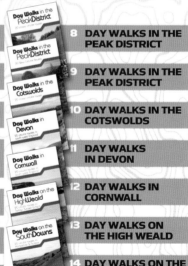

About the Author

Harri Roberts is a freelance writer, editor and translator based in Newport, Gwent. He has authored a number of Welsh walking guides, including an official guide to the Wales Coast Path (Tenby to Swansea section) and a guide to *Day Walks in the Brecon Beacons* (also published by Vertebrate). Together with his partner, Tracy, he has published several electronic walking guides, including an end-to-end hike through Wales (O Fôn i Fynwy), a guide to the England Coast Path between Chepstow and Minehead, and a guide to the Via Algarviana, a long-distance trail across the Algarve region of Portugal.

About the Photographer

Adam Long is a Sheffield-based photographer, specialising in images of wild landscapes, the nature that lives there, and the way people interact with them. His work has been widely published, by publications and clients including *The Times*, National Trust, UKClimbing.com and the British Mountaineering Council. Find out more: **www.adamlong.co.uk**

Vertebrate Publishing

At Vertebrate Publishing we publish books to inspire adventure.

It's our rule that the only books we publish are those that we'd want to read or use ourselves. We endeavour to bring you beautiful books that stand the test of time and that you'll be proud to have on your bookshelf for years to come.

The Peak District was the inspiration behind our first books. Our offices are situated on its doorstep, minutes away from world-class climbing, biking and hillwalking. We're driven by our own passion for the outdoors, for exploration, and for the natural world; it's this passion that we want to share with our readers.

We aim to inspire everyone to get out there. We want to connect readers – young and old – with the outdoors and the positive impact it can have on well-being. We think it's particularly important that young people get outside and explore the natural world, something we support through our publishing programme.

As well as publishing award-winning new books, we're working to make available many out-of-print classics in both print and digital formats. These are stories that we believe are unique and significant; we want to make sure that they continue to be shared and enjoyed.
www.v-publishing.co.uk